Spiritual Authority

Workbook 3

of the series,

Living a Supernatural Life, Naturally

by Linda Morgan

Living a Supernatural Life, Naturally

Spiritual Authority
by Linda Morgan
Part Three of the series, *Living a Supernatural Life, Naturally*

Copyright © 2021 Linda Morgan

Print book ISBN: 978-1-954509-00-9
eBook ISBN: 978-1-954509-03-0

Cover design by VisionRun.com
Photo credit: iStock

Printed in the United States
visionrun.com

About the Author

Linda Morgan is a wife, mother, grandmother, business owner and gifted Christian teacher. She is well known for her ability to express spiritual principles in everyday language. After being introduced to the person of the Holy Spirit in the 1970s, she has spent the years since then studying and sharing what she's learned with others.

She has ministered and taught in churches in the U.S., at retreats, through keynote addresses and on mission trips to Europe and Central America. Linda has also had a personal prayer ministry for hurting people for over thirty years. She is passionate about helping others resolve inner and outer conflict through prayers that heal the heart and change lives.

As a business owner, she also consults and speaks to individuals and professionals alike on the importance of first impressions, and works with clients on wardrobe, color, style and makeup.

Linda and her husband Dell make their home in Knoxville, Tennessee. They have been married for almost fifty years and have two grown children and seven grandchildren.

Table of Contents

Introduction to Living a Supernatural Life Naturally

For about thirty years prior to developing the material for this study I had been involved in leading women's ministries. About 2011 I sensed the Lord was telling me it was time for rest and recharging of my spiritual batteries. It seemed He was telling me it was time to take care of myself physically and build up my spiritual man. I needed a time that involved "being" instead of "doing."

So after pulling back from leading in our church for a season, I sensed the Lord saying it was time to get involved again. I began praying and asking Him what my purpose was now. It seemed He immediately spoke to my heart saying "I want you to teach a Bible Study in the fall. The title is *Living a Supernatural Life Naturally* and here are the ten topics." You can imagine that I immediately felt overwhelmed. But He reminded me that I had already taught most of those subjects over the years.

The purpose of this study is to bring an increased awareness, appreciation for, and understanding of the ministry of the Holy Spirit in our daily lives. The goal is to bring us deeper into His presence through the ministry of the Holy Spirit. We want to develop a listening ear that enables us to respond more readily to the still, quiet voice of the Spirit in our everyday lives.

We can know the Holy Spirit as a Person of the Godhead and not just think of Him as an impersonal influence in our lives. We want to begin to live supernaturally through the power of the Holy Spirit working in us to accomplish God's purposes by fully living the Christ life.

–Linda Morgan

Living a Supernatural Life Naturally Course Overview to Date

Christ delegated spiritual authority to believers; however, it's up to us to exercise that authority
2 Corinthians 10:3-5,8; Luke 9:1, 10:19, 19:17.

Review of topics in the first and second workbooks:

Workbook One:

- **Grace** is not just God's favor; it is also His empowerment to us so that we can overcome our weakness and sin to do His will (Romans 6:14). Everyone who has grace has the Holy Spirit living in him and can live a supernatural life naturally. Jesus wants to live His life through us, as us.

- **The Gift** of the Holy Spirit was sent to us as a Helper. The Holy Spirit is a Person, not just an impersonal influence. Jesus did not leave us helpless (John 14:26, 15:26). Being filled with the Spirit is continual (Ephesians 5:18). Spiritual gifts are supernatural manifestations of God's power provided by the Holy Spirit.

- **Living a Life of Faith** - The gift of faith is like a mustard seed that must be planted, watered, fertilized, protected and pruned. True spiritual life flows from our spirit and affects our mind. Faith is a gift of grace. Faith is taking that first step without seeing what is ahead. Faith occurs when we stop trying to do something by our own efforts and trust someone else to do it for us. Belief and faith are not the same. Acting on our belief means we have faith.

Workbook Two:

- **The Power of Prayer** happens when we believe that God is and that He rewards those who seek Him. Answered prayer affirms us (Hebrews 11:6). We pray because we believe (have faith) and hope that prayer changes things. Prayer is not overcoming God's reluctance but laying hold of His willingness.

- **Listening Prayer** - The Holy Spirit leads and guides us into all truth, but we have to develop a listening ear (John 16:13). God speaks to us both indirectly and directly; He is always speaking, but we are not always listening. God speaks to us and through us (1 Corinthians 12).

- **Obedience** - If we are willing and obedient, we will eat the good of the land (Isaiah 1:19). Obedience brings revelation (John 14:6). It is a key to destiny; it comes faster when we are obedient. Grace empowers us to live a life of obedience, and it empowers us to live beyond our abilities (John 21:15-17).

Living in the age of the New Testament means we are covered by grace and are under a new covenant. A covenant that means we don't have to work and struggle because we can rest in what Christ has provided. *We have the gift of the Holy Spirit, the very presence of Jesus living in us and enabling us to live a supernatural life, naturally.* It requires trusting that He is doing just that, and we don't have to make things happen. We pray, listen, and obey what the Spirit is saying. If we make a mistake and miss it (and sometimes we will), we confess, repent, and ask Him to empower us to do better. He has delegated spiritual authority to us, and when our hearts are right and our motives are pure, we can be effective over the enemy.

Lesson 1: Walk in the Spirit

Spiritual Authority is not worldly power, which is often fueled by insecurity. It is simple delegated authority.

Spiritual authority means having authority over the realm of darkness and Satan's minions. If we don't understand spiritual authority, we won't be effective in spiritual warfare. In fact, we won't know that we can defeat the enemy. We will believe (consciously or subconsciously) that Satan is more powerful than God in our circumstances. Instead of defeating the enemy, we will feel defeated, which will open the door for hopelessness and despair. We can use the name of Jesus to stop the attacks against others and ourselves. Jesus came to give us life — an abundant life **(John 10:10)**.

Spiritual authority is not a tug-of-war on a horizontal plane; when working as designed, it is more like a vertical chain of command. Jesus Christ has all authority in heaven and on earth **(Matthew 28:18)**; He's at the top. He has given His authority and power to His servants to be exercised in His name **(Luke 10:17)**; we're underneath Him. Where does that leave Satan and his demons? They're at the bottom, subject to the authority Christ has given us. Neil Anderson, in the book *The Bondage Breaker*, says they [Satan and his demons] have no more right to rule a believer's life than a buck private has to order a general to clean the latrine. Why then does the kingdom of darkness exert such negative influence in the world and in the lives of Christians? In short, the lie. Satan is not an equal power to God; he is a vanquished foe who was never equal in the first place! But if Satan can deceive you into believing that he has more power and authority than you do, you will live as if he does! Even car pioneer Henry Ford, who was certainly no theologian, was famous for saying, *"Whether you believe you can or you can't — you're right!"* He knew that the main battles in life occur in the mind, not the apparent circumstances of life.

Understanding the spirit realm: Angels are ministering spirits created by God, and they are organized by role, assignment, and rank. Lucifer is a fallen angel **(Daniel 10:13, 20)**.

Similarly, demons are also organized by role, rank, assignment, and power. Satan is the highest ranking angelic created being, and brings temptation to us all. Too often, this world is not a playground but a battleground. But it's a battleground in which our victory is assured. Chip Ingram, in his book, *The Invisible War*, points out that we fight, yes, but we are not fighting from a vulnerable position trying to gain victory; we have God on our side and therefore fight FROM a place of victory already gained.

Spiritual warfare is not an attempt to gain the victory; it is standing firm to defend and keep secure what we already possess. We use spiritual authority to do this.

We must understand that because Satan is a defeated foe and we are in Christ, we are already victorious. The only power Satan has over us is what we give him. **1 John 4:4** says greater is He [Jesus] that is within me than he who is in the world. **Revelation 12:11** says we overcome him by the blood of the Lamb and by the word of our testimony. **James 4:7** says to submit yourselves therefore to God. When encountering a spiritual battle, check your motive, and your heart. Are you yielding your will to God's? Make sure you haven't given Satan access to your life through sin. Then stand firm in God's promises and your God-given authority.

See video clip *"The Gospel"* by Eric Ludy www.ellerslie.com/the-gospel-film/

Man is made in the image of God (Genesis 1:26-27).

When we try to picture or imagine God, we tend to picture Him looking like us. That's only natural. But we know that He is a Spirit, invisible to us and immortal. If we are made in the image of God, we are also spiritual beings, despite what we see in the natural. Just as God is three in one not three beings, man isn't three beings either but has physical, emotional, and spiritual elements. So if this is true, then the picture we present to the world isn't our true image because our true image is invisible to others. Our physical image is confined to this world only, whereas our true image is invisible to the physical eyes and can only be "seen" when one is in the spirit realm, because in Christ, we are new creations. Whereas once we were dead, we are now very much alive. That is why scripture says to know no man after the flesh ("*sarx*" in Greek) but after the spirit (2 Corinthians 5:16-17). Webster's defines "image" as a reproduction or imitation of the form of a person or thing; exact likeness; or semblance. So remember, the next time you catch yourself assuming God is reacting like you would, stop and ask yourself, How is He conforming or transforming you into His image?

Each spirit in each person is unique.

That's why most of the time God speaks to us individually. We each hear and relate to God differently. John 3:6 says that what is born of the flesh is flesh, but what is born of the Spirit is spirit. As believers we are supernatural spirit beings who live in a natural world.

We are all different and individual because God gave each of us a soul. With that we received a will, and we each have different expressions of personality. Our soul belongs to our spirit, not our body. The Spirit is eternal, and the soul expresses the type of spirit we carry in life. The body carries out the dictates of the soul and/or spirit. The conscience is the window between the two.

Man's spirit and soul will live forever and never cease to exist. Scripture says that there is a place prepared for this immortal image of God. Immortal man will exist in that place. Actually, there are two places: heaven and hell. During our time on earth, we choose the place in which we will spend eternity, either with God or separated from God. The decisions we make during our earthly life have eternal consequences.

Man became a living soul when God breathed life into him.

God energized consciousness, which is the realm of the mind and emotions. Life can only come from life — God directly breathed life into man, and he became a living soul. He *spoke* to plants, trees, and animals, but He *breathed life* into man.

The soul is given life by the blood. With thanks to H. A. Maxwell Whyte, author of *The Power of the Blood,* consider the following thoughts on the bloodstream of Jesus, and how biologically speaking, it was not tainted by Adamic blood, even though He was carried by Mary.

- The female ovum itself has no blood, neither has the male spermatozoon; but it is when these come together in the fallopian tube that conception takes place, and a new life begins. The blood cells in this new creation are from both father and mother, and the blood type is determined at the moment of conception. The baby has neither parents' blood, but has its own. The mother's blood does not normally mix with the fetus.

- The Bible is explicit that the Holy Spirit was the Divine Agent who caused Jesus' conception in the womb of Mary. This, therefore, was not a normal conception, but a supernatural act of God in planting the life of His already existing Son right in the womb of Mary, with no normal conception of a male spermatozoon with the female ovum of Mary.

- The placenta produces a number of hormones that are needed during pregnancy, such as lactogen, estrogen and progesterone. It keeps the mother's blood separate from the baby's blood to protect the baby against infections. In fact, if blood from the mother mixes with the baby's blood, it could be fatal for them both.

- As the baby has neither parents' blood, all the Child's blood came from His Father in heaven by a supernatural creative act of God. So Jesus' blood was without the Adamic stain of sin.

- Jesus was the only begotten son of the Father, (John 1:14) and the LIFE that was in Jesus Christ came alone from the Father by the Holy Spirit. No wonder He said, "I am the LIFE" (see John 11:25, 14:6). God imparted His own life into the bloodstream of Jesus. Adamic blood is corrupt and carried by Mary, who declared that Jesus her Son was "God my Savior" (Luke 1:47).

- When a person trusts in Jesus a miracle happens. Immediately, a great cleansing takes place, and the sin that is in the blood stream is purged. For I will cleanse their blood that I have not cleansed; for the Lord dwells in Zion (Joel 3:21).

Could something in our DNA change when we become a Christian?

The soul denotes self, complete with emotions, appetites and volition. It represents our psyche. It encompasses what man was meant to be: *nephesh*, a Hebrew word meaning vital spirit: *soul, self, life, creature, person, appetite, mind, living being, desire, emotion, passion.*

The soul is:

- That which breathes, the breathing substance or being, soul, the inner being of man, living being (with life in the blood), mind (thoughts, conscious, dreams, subconscious, memories)

- Will (ability to choose)

- Emotions and passion (expressing feelings)

- The man himself, self, person or individual, seat of appetites

Our soul allows us to present the glory within us to the atmosphere around us. That is why God says to love Him with our **whole heart** (*kardis*- will and character, center of all physical and spiritual life*)*, **soul** (psyche- life force which animates), **strength** (*ischys*- power, ability) and **mind** (*dianoia*- understanding, feeling, desiring, way of thinking) Luke 10:27. The heart is the reflection of the soul.

&ᷟ *Prayer: Lord, You said to love You with all my heart, soul, strength, and mind. You know I don't love You the way I need to, but You said to do it and I am under grace, so You must have provided a way for me to love You that way. I'm asking You to do that in me. Thank You for helping me to love You that way, Amen.*

Before Adam and Eve sinned, there was no darkness in them.

Perhaps before the Fall, the spiritual and the physical realms were not separated. Did physical laws change after Adam and Eve died spiritually? They lost their spiritual connection to God. Could that have fractured the natural and supernatural into two realms?

Perhaps Adam and Eve were clothed with light before the Fall. We do know that after the Fall something happened to put a veil over man's eyes and heart so he could no longer see God or see into the spiritual dimension that is all around us. So could it be that their light went out, and that is how they knew they were naked and became ashamed? They could hear God, but could no longer see Him. Perhaps their nakedness was evident to them because they were no longer covered in light. They were now living in the other kingdom, the one of darkness.

Discussion:

Do you ever feel as if your light has gone out, and shame keeps you out of the presence of God? Why is that?

The Bible names two trees in the Garden.

- The first, the Tree of Life, relates to the spiritual life that the Lord had breathed into Adam (Genesis 2:9, 16-17). Eating the fruit of this tree would have resulted in eternal life because this tree represents Jesus.

- The second, the Tree of Knowledge, resulted in spiritual death, and related to natural life. Eating this fruit resulted in spiritual death.

The enemy said: *You will not die, but you will become as gods being able to choose for yourselves* **(Genesis 3:4-5).** Eve "ate." That is, claimed she claimed the right to self-rule and shared that rebellion with Adam, who also ate the fruit. We are still paying a terrible price today for mankind trying to become "as gods" and ruling ourselves apart from our Creator.

 A spiritual exercise, such as the following, will be at the end of each lesson, is to help you develop a deeper understanding of grace and strengthen your ability to hear the voice of the Holy Spirit.

God Moment:

Close your eyes and picture…

See yourself reclining under a tree near a quiet spring of water. The Lord Jesus is sitting there with you and He has some things He wants to tell you and some things He wants to give you. Be still and listen, then journal below what you believe He is saying to you.

Now tell Him your fears and concerns. Let Him flood your heart with peace. Ask Him for a revelation of grace.

"Beloved, I have some fruit in my hand; I want you to reach out and receive it. Ask me what the fruit is that I have just for you. I will help you grow your own, if you receive what I have for you now."

Psalms23; 2 Timothy 1:7; Galatians 5:22-23.

Assignment:

Describe situations where it's hard for you to give up self-rule.

_____

_____

_____

List your formulas and self-imposed principles.

_____

_____

_____

What are you afraid will happen if you don't perform?

_____

_____

_____

In the past, how have you understood the difference between soul and spirit? Have you had any new insights?

_____

_____

_____

Final thought:

The breath of God gives me life, so the life I now live in the body, I live by faith in the Son of God, who loved me and gave himself for me (Galatians 2:20).

_____

_____

_____

_____

_____

_____

_____

_____

_____

_____

_____

_____

_____

_____

_____

_____

_____

_____

_____

_____

_____

_____

Lesson 2: Walk in Grace

Because of disobedience Adam and Eve lost their spiritual connection to God.

After they sinned by eating the fruit, the Lord came to walk with Adam, who had hidden from His presence. Adam said he hid because he was *naked*. He had lost the "Shekinah covering" or divine light that enabled him to abide in the manifest presence and glory of the Lord.

In the Old Testament, the Most Holy Place within the Tabernacle was where the manifest presence of God resided. It is a picture of the Holy Spirit in us.

At Pentecost, the fire that came on the men and women in the upper room reminds us of the fire over the Most Holy Place in the Tabernacle. This is where God dwelt. It lit up the darkness. Now that fire is over us because He dwells in us and we are called to be the light in the darkness.

Through Christ, the Lord has brought us back into a cooperative, personal relationship with Himself that was lost in the Garden of Eden.

Arise, shine; for your light is come, and the glory of the Lord is risen upon you. For, behold, the darkness shall cover the earth, and gross darkness the people: but the Lord shall arise upon you, and His glory shall be seen upon you. And the Gentiles shall come to your light, and kings to the brightness of your rising (Isaiah 60:1-3).

2 Corinthians 4:6-7 says *For God, who said, "Let light shine out of darkness," made his light shine in our hearts to give us the light of the knowledge of God's glory displayed in the face of Christ. But we have this treasure in jars of clay to show that this all-surpassing power is from God and not from us.*

It was God's mercy to expel Adam and Eve from the Garden — because they might have eaten from the Tree of Life and lived forever in their sinful state. Since Jesus is our Tree of Life we can enter the presence of God. Taking communion, eating His flesh and drinking His blood, symbolizes our new covenant **(John 6:55; 1 Corinthians 11:25)**.

A kingdom requires three things.

A kingdom requires three things: a territory, a ruler, and those who are ruled over. Jesus is the King, but He will rule only those who have personally given Him permission to do so. We must give up the right for self-rule that came into the carnal nature at the Fall when Adam and Eve ate of the Tree of the Knowledge of Good and Evil.

Religion is self-rule and self-effort.

You may have heard people say they are spiritual, but not religious. Or you may have known people who were extremely religious, but not particularly spiritual. There is a huge difference between the two terms, even though they are often used interchangeably. Religion was introduced when Adam and Eve tried to cover themselves. They lost their intimate relationship with God, spirit-to-Spirit **(Genesis 3:7-11)**.

Religion rules out grace and robs relationship.

Religion requires legalistic rule-keeping that leads to spiritual death. It means our confidence is in self-effort expressed through formulas and principles, not in a trusting relationship with the Holy Spirit to work in us to accomplish His purposes.

"Religion" in this sense grows out of our insecurity and produces a sense of false security because it seems easier to make and keep rules than to be led by the Spirit. Once again, it leads us in a direction of self-dependence and self-rule, and it robs us of intimacy with God.

If you tend to be a rule-follower, you may think that keeping rules causes you to stay in good standing with God, or it might be your way of showing love or obedience to God. But that's not true! Our good standing comes from being in Christ. God wants a relationship, i.e., give and take, communion with us. Robotically following additional rules tells God, "What You did isn't enough, so I'll do more." Ridiculous, right?

Self-imposed rules will keep us from trusting God; when we do that, we step out of grace.

When we understand the grace that flowed down to us from the Cross, we will know that Jesus' sacrifice is enough. We don't need to add anything to what He has already done for us. **It is finished!**

Some churches promote religion more than relationship. You cannot expect a deep level of ministry to happen in your life or the lives of the people when the outward appearance is more important than being transparent about your feelings. Churches like that foster the fear that if you don't conform to the expectations of "holiness" you will be rejected. Because you have to keep up a facade, you can never be transparent. If, as a result, something stays hidden in darkness, it will thrive and grow in a way that is destructive to you and those around you.

Discussion:

If you had a legalistic upbringing, how does it affect the way you see God?

Legalism is the result of living in the realm of the soul/mind and not from the spirit realm.

Bad root = bad fruit. Legalism is rooted in self-effort and brings a false sense of security. When you are wrapped up in legalism and religion, your conscience is affected. Our conscience is our measure of agreement between our conduct and the values to which we are committed. This bases one's spiritual life on following rules without any change of heart. Therefore when the conscience is dulled, the heart is also hardened to the truth, leaving no room for grace. Cults in particular capitalize on this tendency, and encourage it throughout their membership.

We have been redeemed.

After the Fall, the earth was cursed; thorns became a sign of the curse. Jesus' crown of thorns symbolized that He redeemed man from that curse, and that the earth will be redeemed. He took the curse upon Himself. To redeem means *to pay the required price, to secure the release of a convicted criminal* **(Galatians 3:13; Revelation 22:3).**

Discussion:

How does Jesus redeeming us from the curse affect us?

Psalms 16:11 says He will show us the path of life; in your presence is fullness of joy; at your right hand (place of strength and authority) are pleasures forevermore. When you say someone is your right hand person, what are you saying about that person? It represents a strength, dependability, and power, knowing what you want done and how to do it. You can trust him because you know he has your back.

Luke 22:69 says Jesus is seated at the right hand of the power of God.

Ephesians 2:6 says we are seated with Him in the heavenly places. What that says about us is that we have been given a place of authority in the spirit realm and that Jesus has our back and not just when we get to heaven, but here. Now. Today **(Luke 9:1, 10:19)**.

Redemption is a recurring theme throughout the Bible. "*Padah*" is a Hebrew word that expresses the redemptive concept in relation to the redemption of persons or other living beings **(Exodus 21:29-30, 32)**. "*Ga'al*" is another Hebrew word that indicates a redemptive price in relation to family members involving the responsibility of next of kin. In **Leviticus 25:25, 47-48** we see it was a kinsman's responsibility to ransom [redeem] a relative who had sold his possessions or himself to slavery. In **Ruth 4:4** the need for redemption was the result of poverty. The kinsman was responsible to redeem the estate that his nearest relative might have sold or lost. That is what Jesus did for us. He is our kinsman-redeemer.

Good news: The Lord has redeemed us, that is, bought us and paid our debt in full. We are empowered by His Holy Spirit to walk in the freedom He purchased for us.

If you have never asked Jesus to come into your heart and live His life through you, pray the following prayer:[1]

🔖 *Prayer: Lord Jesus, I repent of going my own way. I ask you to forgive all my sins. I ask you to come into my heart and live your life through me, as me. As I give my life to you, I confess that you are Lord. Amen* **(Romans 10:9)**.

---

1 Once you have prayed that prayer, go tell someone that you have been translated out of the kingdom of darkness into the kingdom of light **(Colossians 1:12-14)**.

Father, I thank you that I am now alive in Christ and free from the power of the enemy. I thank you that your Holy Spirit now lives in me. Amen

The Gift:

The Holy Spirit is the ultimate gift to the church empowering us to live life supernaturally…naturally. **Romans 8:2** *for the law of the Spirit of life in Christ Jesus has made me free from the law of sin and death. This is a supernatural, spiritual exchange.* The Spirit is the dynamic of a believer's experience that leads us into liberty and the power to do God's will. It does not depend on our strength because His strength is made perfect in our weakness **(2 Cor. 2:9)**. The Holy Spirit leads us so we don't need to be in control. We can yield our will to God's will.

When Satan introduced doubt, causing the Fall, Adam and Eve's minds became carnal in nature. Their worldview changed; their spirits no longer influenced their decisions. They were not living supernaturally anymore but naturally. **Romans 8:7** says the *carnal mind* is enmity against God, for it is not subject to the law of God, nor can it be. The Greek word for carnal is "*sarx*" meaning: *the natural mind or flesh.* It denotes mere human nature, the earthly nature of man apart from divine influence, and therefore prone to sin and opposed to God.

Colossians 1:21 describes those who are unregenerate as enemies in the mind and therefore alienated from God. The unregenerate mind is the stronghold of Satan. The mind of the Christian is also the strategic center of the war on the saints. So the battle is still for the mind because the mind is the vehicle for the Spirit of God who dwells in the spirit of the believer **(2 Corinthians 10:3-5)**.

It is through our regenerate spirit that the Spirit of God transmits to us His Truth. Truth will remove the deceptions of Satan. So if the mind is the outlet used to express Jesus to those living in darkness, it must be continually renewed or, like faulty plumbing, your "pipes" will become clogged and you will be ineffective in bearing spiritual fruit. The Holy Spirit *renews* your spirit; the Word *washes* your mind **(Titus 3:5)**.

When we are redeemed, our spirit is delivered from the grip of the enemy but not our mind. That is an ongoing process that we must choose to allow. That is why some Christians never bear fruit. The truth of God's Word cannot get through the clogged pipes (strongholds) in their mind. Their mind has never been fully delivered from whatever hold the enemy has over it.

> *They get a new heart but they keep their old heads.*
> — C.S. Lewis

According to **Ephesians 4:22-23** there has to be a deliberate putting off of the old nature. The body will follow the dictates of the mind, which should be ruled by our spirit. Your emotions will eventually follow as well. But it all starts by a submission of your will to His, in your *mind.*

🌿 *Prayer: Lord, I ask you to show me the areas where my mind still needs to be renewed. Show me the places where I have wrong thinking and am deceived. Open my eyes to any lies I'm believing and reveal truth. Help me to renew my mind in your word.* **Job 13:22** *says if I call on you, you will answer. Thank you Lord, in Christ's name I pray. Amen.*

Dr. Caroline Leaf is a cognitive neuroscientist with a Ph.D. in Communication Pathology, specializing in Neuropsychology. In her book, *Switch on Your Brain,* she says the following:

Your collective thoughts form your attitude, which is your state of mind, and it's your attitude and not your DNA that determines much of the quality of your life.

This state of mind is a real, physical, electromagnetic, quantum, and chemical flow in the brain that switches groups of genes on or off in a positive or negative direction based on your choices and subsequent reactions. Scientifically, this is called epigenetics; spiritually, this is the enactment of Deuteronomy 30:19, *"I have set before you life, death, blessings and cursing; therefore choose life, that both you and your descendants may live." The brain responds to your mind by sending these neurological signals throughout the body, which means that your thoughts and emotions are transformed into physiological and spiritual effects, and then physiological experience transforms into mental and emotional states.*

Discussion:

How do you make difficult decisions — by praying and being led by your spirit or by reasoning with your mind?

God Moment:

Put on some quiet worship music and listen for God to speak to you. Be sure to journal what you feel He is saying.

"Beloved, come into my presence and let my light shine upon you. I want to change your countenance with my glory. Sit at my feet and listen as I tell you how I feel about you. When you grasp how much I love you, your face will shine like Moses' face after spending time with me on the mountaintop and at the tent of meeting.

I want to bring you to the mountaintop and elevate you above your circumstances so you can see what I am doing on your behalf in the heavenly supernatural realm. Lift your face to me and receive all I have for you today."

Praise Him for bringing you out of darkness and into His marvelous light.

2 Corinthians 4:6; 1 Peter 2:9

Assignment:

What are the self-imposed rules you live by?

_____

_____

_____

How did your upbringing affect how you see God?

_____

_____

_____

What causes you to feel powerless?

_____

_____

_____

Final thought:

God wants us to be led supernaturally by the Holy Spirit living in us so we can be effective in the natural realm.

Lesson 3: Walk in the Light

In John 20:21-22 Jesus first told the disciples to spread the gospel, and then He breathed on them and said to receive the Holy Spirit. These are related actions because it is the Holy Spirit's life in us that accomplishes the spreading of the gospel. In Mark 16:15 He told them to spread the gospel to the four corners of the earth. 2 Timothy 3:16 says all scripture is breathed out or inspired by God. The Holy Spirit is often referred to as the Breath of God. Acts 1:8 says they would receive power when the Holy Spirit came upon them. The word used there for the Holy Spirit is *Pneuma Halgion*, which means *Most Holy Thing*. It denotes spiritual power and impartation from on high, without which we cannot be effective, because that is what makes us supernatural (Matthew 5:14).

Our light has been turned back on.

Jesus tells us we are the light of the world, so our lives should allow the world to see something different in us. Our countenance should reflect the light within. However, we are living in darkness when we try to follow self-imposed or religious rules to make us acceptable to God. Instead, we are to be living out of a relationship with a loving Father.

God has spoken His divine light into our spiritual darkness. This happens because of God's grace, Jesus' sacrifice, and our faith in Jesus' promises to cover our sins. The enemy can lie to you all day but if you know in your "knower" that you are forgiven because of grace through faith, Satan will not be able to make you ineffective. This is spiritual truth. In the physical world, light can dispel darkness, but darkness can't dispel light. It can only yield to it. Christ's light will shine through you, especially in this dark world (1 Peter 2:9).

Christ Jesus lives in us; He is our very breath.

He is the light of the world that lives in us, and He is the Word. Remember, God spoke the world into being. Can you speak without using your breath? In **John 20:21-22** Jesus first told the disciples to spread the gospel, and then He breathed on them and said to receive the Holy Spirit. **2 Timothy 3:16** says all scripture is breathed out or inspired by God. **Acts 1:8** says they would receive power when the Holy Spirit came upon them. It denotes spiritual power and impartation from on high, without which we cannot be effective because that is what makes us supernatural.

Ephesians 1:18 talks about "the eyes of your understanding" being "filled with light." In **1 Corinthians 2:13-14** we see that the mind is supposed to be illuminated by the [light of the] Spirit.

These concepts of light, word, and breath are all keys to understanding the authority you have been given to be a light and use the powerful name of Jesus to speak (claim) your authority through the Holy Spirit (breath) living in you.

1 Peter 1:13 talks about girding up the loins of the mind, which means to keep your mind sharp, in shape and aware or on guard. But this can be misconstrued by young Christians who mistakenly believe that their battles are theirs alone. In their hearts they really think it has something to do with their own ability, not His. That's why the scripture says His strength is made perfect in our weakness **(Hebrews 11:34; 2 Corinthians 12:10)**.

It's His power and strength, not ours.

We have been delegated authority in the spiritual realm.

Genesis 1:26-28, 2:15 tells us that God gave Adam legal authority to have dominion over the earth. God put him in the garden and told him to *keep* it, or in Hebrew, "*shamar*" it, which means to protect or guard it like a watchman. It is the same concept as having power of attorney. When someone has power of attorney, they have the power to legally represent the person who gave it to them.

The name of Jesus is our power of attorney. The Holy Spirit is our seal. In biblical days, when subjects saw the seal of a king or someone in authority over them, they knew they had to obey what was written. The same is true today in the spiritual realm; when the enemy sees the seal of the Holy Spirit on us as we speak the Word of God using the name of Jesus, he must obey (2 Corinthians 1:22; Ephesians 1:13).

The Significance of the Blood

Jesus's blood was pure, without the stain of sin from the Fall (Matthew 1:18; John 1:14). Since He was begotten by the Father, there was none of Adam's blood in His veins. Even though Mary carried Him, His blood came from His Father, God, by the Holy Spirit.[2] It was full of light and life. The blood is powerful because it covers (that is, pays for) our sin. After The Fall, Satan owned us all, because we share Adam's blood. Now we belong to Christ.

The blood of Jesus is the reason we have spiritual authority. If you are a believer, the blood of Jesus covers you, but you must appropriate it. An example of appropriating the blood in our lives would be a prayer something like, "*Lord I thank you that the blood covers my sin, thus, the enemy has no legal right to accuse me.*" We do this naturally when we take communion.

---

2 Biologically, there is no blood in the ovum; and the fetus's blood is formed after conception, independent of the mother.

There is power in the name of Jesus because He shed His own blood and offered it to His Father. The Father gave Jesus His power and authority (Matthew 28:18). That same power God gave Jesus is delegated to us when we appropriate the name and the blood (Luke 10:19).

Revelation 12:11 says they overcame the enemy by the word of their testimony and the blood of the Lamb. We appropriate the blood by faith. The blood of Jesus has sprinkled us (Hebrews 9:7-14, 10:19-22). When Jesus carried his blood and sprinkled it on the original altar in heaven that was the final act of atonement ever needed. God himself made the atonement. *He did what we could never do.* Once we appropriate His sacrifice on the doorpost of our hearts, we do not have to fear Satan ever again. It is finished. Praise God!

Prayer: Lord, I thank you that the blood of Jesus covers me, and Satan has no legal right to harass or oppress me. I take authority over the oppressing spirit of fear, or insecurity, or jealousy, or sickness, or anger, or unbelief, or whatever else it might be, in the name of Jesus and command it to leave me alone.

I repent of anything I may have done to open the door to this harassment and oppression. I forgive anyone who has hurt or offended me. Through confessing, repenting, and forgiving, I close the door to Satan and cancel his assignment against me. Thank you, Lord. In Jesus' name I pray. Amen.

Deception is Satan's greatest weapon.

- If Satan can keep us from understanding everything salvation means for us, we are ineffective. Then demons don't have to fear us.

- When we believe that God is the source of everything bad that happens in our life, we open ourselves to deception. Satan is god of this world, and we have freedom of choice, so while God is all-powerful, He will not interrupt our freedom of choice, and Satan will wreak havoc if he can get us to believe that what happens due to our own poor choices is or was God's will.

- When we agree with Satan's lies, we can be deceived about ourselves and about others. It changes our relationships with God and with each other.

We do not have any natural ability, but we have supernatural empowerment, which makes us more than able to overcome the enemy (John 15:4-5).

Psalms 8:3-6 says that God gave man dominion. Dominion is the English translation of the word "*mashal*" meaning ruler, manager, steward, representative, go-between, or mediator. Taking dominion means to occupy the space or land God has allotted to us, to take possession and drive out enemies. The Garden was Adam and Eve's space to rule because God planted them there, and His delegation to them [command] of "dominion" meant to extend the garden and multiply Eden over the whole earth.

Discussion:

So what would it look like to extend Eden? What would earth have looked like? (Isaiah 11:6, 65:25).

What are you creating with your dominion? As we've established, words are powerful — both God's word and our own. Think of your words in daily conversation like seeds being sown in a garden.

Are you sowing words that will produce faith, or are you sowing words of doubt? The seeds (words) you sow are meant to grow into fruit that will nourish and sustain you, but you can dig up your own seed by speaking words of doubt and unbelief contrary to what God has spoken to you, and contrary to what scripture says.

Adam could choose life or death.

Adam was given a choice about whether or not to exercise free will and love God in response to God's love for him. Being made in the image of God means (among other attributes) having free will. God didn't want a bunch of little robots running around with no choice about whether or not to obey Him.

Everything was provided for Adam — food, shelter, work to do, and even a mate with whom to share all the glory of creation. Loving and obeying God was supposed to be part of a pure, loving relationship. True love must be mutual. It involves being free to choose with our own will to love God in response to His love. It is a choice based on trust — trust that God has our best interests at heart. John 10:10 says it is *the enemy who comes to steal, kill and destroy but Jesus came to give us abundant life.*

We were created to glorify God by being relational with God and each other. In the Garden, those relationships came through a pure heart. There were no self-serving or other wrong motives because sin hadn't entered the picture.

Believing Satan's lies in the Garden caused Adam and Eve to doubt God, giving an open door to sin and disobedience. This changed their relationship with God and with each other. Now the lens through which they viewed life was stained by sin, and they could no longer see clearly.

Even today, with the love of Christ in our hearts, when we believe Satan's lies, our relationship with God and with others will be affected.

Adam and Eve lost their right to rule.

You've heard of decisions having unintended consequences. And in fact, we almost never know the full extent of the results of our choices in life at the time we make them. But we are responsible for them nonetheless. When Adam and Eve made the choice to disobey, whether they realized it or not at the time, they were giving their authority — their dominion — of the earth to Satan. Through their disobedience, they forfeited their influence over creation and gave it to Satan by coming into agreement with the enemy. When we agree with the enemy's lies, we give him power over us.

Demons depend on Christians to lower the barrier God has placed around them. The barrier is our individual sovereign will. They will use lies, tricks, deceptions, or any other underhanded means by which to defeat us because they can't touch us unless we allow it. You can see a great explanation of this concept throughout C.S. Lewis's classic book, *The Screwtape Letters*. The bottom line is that when Adam sinned, he joined Satan's rebellion against God.

Satan became a defeated foe at Calvary and only has the power over us that we give him.

In Luke 10:17-20 Jesus tells us He saw Satan fall from heaven. Because Jesus cleansed the original altar in heaven (Hebrews 9:23-24), Satan is the accuser, but because he was cast out of heaven, I don't believe he still has the right to go before the throne of God and accuse us. When we are spiritually born again as Christians, Jesus' blood covers us, and we are made righteous. We have become blameless (1 John 1:7; 1 Corinthians 1:8; Ephesians 1:7-8, 5:27; Jude 1:24). Satan tries to accuse us, but he no longer does it before God. Now, his tactic is to accuse us to each other and bring thoughts of accusation to our minds.

Discussion:

If God sees you as blameless, and Satan accuses you as guilty — who are you going to believe? Why is that often a difficult choice?

Unlike Job, who needed an advocate, we have Jesus as our Advocate.

In the Book of Job, Satan is first designated by name, which in Hebrew, means *one who lies in wait; an adversary in a court of justice* (1 Chronicles 21:1; Psalms109:6; Zechariah 3:1); *accuser* (Revelation 12:10). He has the law of God on his side because of man's sin. But Jesus Christ has fulfilled the law for us; justice is once more on man's side against Satan (Isaiah 42:1-3). Jesus Christ can plead as our Advocate against the adversary. "*Devil*" is the Greek name — meaning the "slanderer," or "accuser." He is subject to God, who uses him for chastising man. He is called prince of this world (John 12:31), the god of this world (2 Corinthians 4:4), and the prince of the power of the air (Ephesians 2:2).

Discussion:

How do you know when your thoughts originate with you or the enemy? Does it bring conviction or condemnation, hope or hopelessness? Ask the Lord to help you distinguish between truth and lies.

John 10 tells us that we are capable of hearing the voice of God. He speaks to His sheep…they hear and follow Him (John 10:4). He has not come to condemn the world, but to save the world (John 3:16-17).

Since conviction and condemnation are very much alike, many sincere Christians suffering from condemnation think they are under conviction.

Conviction by the Holy Spirit

- Definite and specific. The Lord tells me exactly what I have done.

- Recognizable. It is something I have not confessed or forgiven that I recognize – usually in the immediate past.

- There is a definite solution.

- The Holy Spirit tells me how to take care of the sin.

- When I obey, I get relief from feeling miserable – I feel lighter.

Condemnation by the Enemy

- I feel guilty but cannot identify any specific sin.

- Imaginary guilt — I have a hard time putting my finger on this unless it is something in the past that I have already taken care of.

- There is usually no solution to the problem. If any solution is offered, it is irrational and unscriptural. The soul-pain intensifies.

- I feel hopeless.

God Moment:

Put on some quiet worship music and listen for God to speak to you. Be sure to journal what you feel He is saying.

"My child, your sins were judged on the cross, now you are found not guilty. Keep your heart pure by confessing any known sin, forgive others, then come before me confident that I will extend my scepter and receive you into my Presence. If there is anything you need to take care of I will bring it to your mind and show you what to do.

"The veil has been torn. This means you can come and open your heart so I can pour out my love and healing balm to your soul and spirit. You have been counted among the Beloved and are acceptable in my sight.

"I want to shower you with my love. Look up and feel the gentle cleansing rain of my Spirit falling upon you. Dance before me in the rain like a little child."

Luke 17:4; Acts 2:38; Esther 8:4; 2 Corinthians 3:16

Assignment:

What has God given you to steward or to mediate spiritually?

_____

_____

_____

What would that mean to you and to your family?

_____

_____

_____

What are his promises to you?

_____

_____

_____

Final thought:

Satan only has the power over us that we give him.

Lesson 4: Walk in Truth

Adam and Eve believed the lie that God didn't know or want what was best for them. The seed of doubt and lack of trust toward a loving Father was planted in the heart of mankind. That is when man began to shift blame and not take ownership or personal responsibility for sin. Adam blamed Eve and she blamed the serpent.

Having choices involves responsibility, and they didn't want to own their bad choices. As a result, Satan gained legal entry into man's thought life in a way that would hinder his destiny.

If you believe Satan's lies, it will become bad fruit in your life.

Discussion:

What are some examples of bad fruit in a person's life as a result of believing lies?

The result of man becoming spiritually separated from God

A veil was formed over the heart and mind of man that would separate him from God. We see a picture of this spiritual veil in the physical, natural realm in the Tabernacle. The Old Testament details how the curtain between the Holy Place and the Holy of Holies separated the priests from the presence of God.

Israel had to have a sacrificial lamb, but Jesus became our sacrificial lamb. Through the cross, we can be cleansed of sin and washed in the Word. We can experience all the beauty God has for us in the spiritual realm.

Today, we don't have to have priests interceding on our

behalf; we have Jesus. We are so blessed that we serve a personal, relational God who is a loving Father and actually lives in each of us. Wow, it's hard to wrap your mind around that **(John 17)**.

Deception and rebellion are Satan's tools.

Regardless of what Satan did to encourage or even instigate it, Adam's sin is what gave Satan legal entry into man's thought life. His decision to disobey was then based from a sin nature, not by the Spirit of God. We refer to that as the flesh. Walking in the flesh is also referred to as the "soulish" realm.

After we are born again, we can still open the door to Satan through sin or disobedience, and he still uses deception to encourage us to do so. Many times he's successful because we don't really trust God to either know what is best for us or to do what is best. Other times it may be ignorance, because we haven't asked God or put forth the effort to get to know Him and deepen our relationship **(2 Corinthians 4:4)**.

Strongholds

Since the Fall, our minds, even as Christians, can be influenced by the demonic and open to strongholds and vain imaginings **(2 Corinthians 10:3-5)**. A stronghold is a thought process impregnated by a spiritual force that keeps a person in bondage.

The foundation of a stronghold is a belief system or mind-set that is opposed to the truth of God.

Knowledge of God means "a living and interactive experience," not a theoretical or merely intellectual understanding of God. But too often, our minds and our culture are opposed to the knowledge of God.

In this fallen world, man has a new filter distorting his vision. Being expelled from the Garden is a picture of this. Rather than seeing the beauty of creation, people saw the effects of sin everywhere. Our lives are generally governed by the five senses and human logic (the mind) instead of a spirit to Spirit connection with God. That's contrary to our original design; it affects our attitude toward life, God, the world, the future, and each other. When circumstances rule your thinking, you make decisions without consulting God first. With Christ, we have a direct spiritual pipeline to God. However, sin, unforgiveness, or wrong thinking can clog it up.

Our *attitude* often determines our spiritual *altitude*. A bad attitude is one big way our spiritual connection can become blocked. Consider chickens and eagles — they're both birds, but have very different perspectives. Which one are you most like? Do you live in the chicken yard, or soar like an eagle? An eagle has the ability to see the whole picture from above, which gives it a discernment a chicken can never have. All the chicken sees is the ground under them. It can't see the snake trying to get into the hen house. Let your attitude be such that you think and see more like an eagle, and you'll be much closer to seeing God's perspective. Let Him lift your life as you lift your perspective.

Without discernment it is impossible to be effective spiritually. We need God's wisdom and understanding to destroy our true enemies; otherwise, we will mistake our fellow Christians as enemies and destroy them instead. We have to rise above our circumstances, which is hard to do unless the Holy Spirit gives us discernment.

Satan wants our thought lives and feelings to control our actions rather than for us to be controlled by what God says in His word. Satan's goal is to shut down our spirit by using our minds and bodies to control our decisions. Just like with Eve, he wants to cause doubt in our minds about the goodness of God and to make us question if the word of God is true. He will attack God's character and try to bring us along to do the same, either actively or passively.

We act out of what we believe, not what we "know."

Satan targets our weaknesses.

He tries to defeat us through the areas of our life not yet redeemed:

- Emotions
- Trauma
- Illness
- Intellect

He uses our weaknesses to influence our relationships with others and with God. Ephesians 6:12 says we are not wrestling against flesh and blood. This is a spiritual battle.

In Numbers 22:5-7, when Balak hired Balaam to curse Israel, God would not allow him to do it. So instead, Balaam told them to lure the men of Israel into sexual sin by tempting them with the Moabite women. The women then led them into idolatry, (Numbers 31:18; Revelation 2:14) and with this strategy, he was successful. He targeted their weakness and caused them to bring a curse on themselves (Numbers 25:1-11). In the same way, Satan will try first one way and then another, targeting each of our weaknesses as he tries to gain access into our lives. Anything to kill, steal, or destroy.

When we allow strongholds to stay in our lives unhealed they become access points for evil spirits to enter and cause more trouble. Evil spirits access strongholds protecting wrong attitudes, patterns of thinking, beliefs and behaviors. We can bind an evil spirit from the source of vulnerability in a human soul, but the vulnerability also has to be dealt with or similar spirits will come. Then our minds become controlled by wrong thoughts. An example of this would be to constantly question your salvation and be tormented by doubt about whether or not you're really a Christian. A legalistic spirit feeds this.

There can be vulnerability to a particular kind of spirit because of strongholds (unbelief, pride, deception, addiction, guilt, unforgiveness, sexual strongholds, etc…) Therefore, Satan will constantly lead a person through situations and circumstances that will put them around such like spirits. This cycle can continue almost without end, so the doorway of access, that is, the stronghold itself, must be destroyed.

An example of a wrong attitude stronghold that would give access would be to think that divorce is an option if marriage is hard. Other patterns of thinking might be about money, performance-driven behavior, or even religious works (legalism). A person who becomes controlled in any of these areas might have a demonic spirit driving them. Sometimes it can look like and seem to be a "good thing." A person driven by good works, for instance, would fall into this category. The focus on works could be driven by a spirit of legalism, not the Holy Spirit.

Discussion:

Can you think of other ways the enemy can gain access to a person's life?

Proverbs 4:23 says out of the heart spring the issues of life. If a person believes he is sickly and weak, that will open the door to a spirit of infirmity reinforcing that wrong belief. Rebuking a spirit and telling it to go will not bring total freedom because if the stronghold it is protecting is not dealt with, a similar spirit will enter the person's mind or body or emotions, and re-establish access, increasing the attack.

For example, if a stronghold of guilt is dealt with but a revelation of forgiving yourself doesn't happen, a spirit of shame will then set up shop. Rebuking will deactivate a demon's power temporarily. But if believing a lie opened the door in the first place, the Lord needs to speak truth to replace the lie so the person can go forward.[3]

The lie might be that people won't like you if they really know you or realize you're not perfect. For example, if you had an abortion and you know that God has forgiven you, but there is still shame and condemnation, those feelings will keep you in bondage. Also, if you don't forgive yourself and whoever else had a part in it, you will stay imprisoned by the sin.

We have to be healed in our emotions of the past to move into our future.

One must be honest about the emotions associated with painful memories and not make excuses for those who were involved. Our emotions are tied to the past; to the way we operate, with whom we operate, and why we had problems in a previous situation. Certain things might trigger an extreme emotional response in us, and we don't know why we have overreacted. Your will is involved in that. You must choose to deal with the pain.

Prayer: Lord, help me to be honest with myself about painful memories. Help me to be able to face the truth. Show

---

3 For more detail on healing prayer, see Workbook 5 in this series.

me why I overreact in certain situations and help me to forgive anyone who caused any of the traumas. Psalms34:18 says the Lord is near to the broken hearted and saves the crushed in spirit. Thank you Lord for hearing my prayer, Amen.

If you want to live a supernatural life naturally and exercise spiritual authority, you have to deal with whatever keeps you from being confident that God is on your side.

Forgiveness is essential to moving forward and receiving emotional healing.

God Moment:

Be still and listen for God to speak to you. Be sure to journal what you feel He is saying.

Listen as the Lord tells you what strongholds of wrong thinking He wants to remove from your mind. Ask Him how you have been deceived in the way you think and how you see certain things. Now picture the chains of wrong thinking being cut off.

Ask Him how He sees you and what He thinks about you. Now if there is anyone you are having difficulty loving, ask the Lord to show you His heart toward him or her, and how He sees that person.

2 Kings 6:20; 2 Chronicles 7:15; Psalms 119:18; 1 Peter 3:12

Assignment:

What are your areas of weakness that Satan targets?

_____

_____

_____

Ask the Lord to show you any areas where you are deceived.

_____

_____

_____

From the strongholds mentioned in this lesson, which do you struggle with the most and why?

_____

_____

_____

Do you have some physical issues that could be caused by emotional stress?

_____

_____

_____

Final thought:

Jesus came to set the captives free.

Journal

_____

_____

_____

_____

_____

_____

_____

_____

_____

_____

Lesson 5: Walk in Freedom

Traumas in your past can produce paralyzing fear, a sense of failure, complex emotional distress, and anxiety. Joy and freedom come back when we invite Jesus to come into those dark, painful places and speak truth to the lies we believed as a result of the trauma. Outside of Christ, a person's spirit is deadened and controlled by the world, but in Christ that same spirit is alive and joyful, flowing like a river out to the world (John 7:37-39).

The enemy wants to block our emotions.

When our emotions are blocked, they become stagnant, like standing water with no outlet, a breeding ground for disease and decay. Quite simply, when our emotions are dammed up, our river of life within is blocked.

Blocked emotions can literally make us sick, causing our organs to overwork (especially the spleen, kidneys and pancreas) and even create adrenal failure. It's like someone who has a chronic sinus infection due to something blocking his or her ability to drain so that it requires surgery to remove the problem. Inner healing is like the surgery.

When not processed correctly, trauma will shape your world from the point of view of the hurtful situation and circumstance that was experienced, and as a result strongholds are formed.

Satan takes advantage of traumas by creating victim mentalities and confused perspectives within us, which produce dullness, deadness, lost hope, apathy, anxiety and blocked emotions. It can weaken the spirit (Proverbs 18:14).

A broken spirit occurs when life's difficulties crush our ability to resist.

The enemy wants to minimize our life in the Spirit so we go from supernaturally flowing to being naturally isolated and stagnated. But Jesus came to give us abundant life flowing from us to others. Satan uses blame and guilt, somehow making us believe bad things that happen to us are deserved, or that they are our fault.

We reverse Satan's process by breaking the stronghold, releasing us from destructive behavior and a wrong pattern of thinking to expose the actual hurt beneath all those layers so that God can heal it (2 Corinthians 10:4). We *must choose to* correct wrong ideas, shatter and dissolve evil imaginations, wrong theories, reasoning, and thoughts.

Wrong desires come from unmet needs, so through repentance we remove those wrong desires along with the strongholds that surround them. Repent for looking to anyone but the Lord to meet your needs.

Prayer: Lord, I bind my mind to the mind of Christ. I bind my mind to the truth of God's word. I bind my will to the will of God.

I bind my feet to the path God has for me. I loose my mind from every deception, every hindering spirit, every stronghold and vain imagining that would keep me from walking in the destiny God has for my life (Matthew 18:18).

I would suggest that you pray this daily for yourself or for someone else whose name you insert. When you see results, begin to thank God for what He's done.

Only bind yourself to the absolute known things of God found within His Word. His will, the blood of Jesus, the mind of Christ, the truth of His Word, paths of righteousness, the work of the cross, and God's timing.
— Liberty Savard

We forgive from our spirit; we attempt to cover over unforgiveness through our soul. We feel justified in our unwillingness to forgive because we think we are right. When you have unforgiveness, ask God to change your heart.

Satan dines on what we withhold from God.
—Francis Frangipane, *The Three Battlefields*

Crucify the old nature and make room for the new.

Loosing old wrong attitudes, patterns of thinking, ideas and beliefs, and the strongholds protecting them is the surest, fastest way to accomplish crucifying the old nature and making room for the new. Deception gives way to temptation and results in bondage. Truth brings deliverance, which brings freedom.

When there are misunderstandings, bind Satan, the strongman, and loose his deceptions that were impacting the situation. Sometimes we need to loose the power and effects of words spoken against us or by us.

Prayer: Lord, in the name of Jesus I cancel every demonic assignment against me. I command the oppressive spirits of darkness attacking my mind and emotions to stop and leave me now. Thank you Father for setting me free John 8:36.

Freedom comes when we bind our mind and will to the truth and loose old wrong habits and beliefs, attitudes, thinking, desires and behavior in our life. Strongholds need to be dealt with because they blind men's minds so that the light of the gospel cannot shine through.

Repentance is the key to unlock the door of our heart.

> *Embrace me, Eternity*
>
> *Let your horizon expand within me*
>
> *Melt the chains of my inner man*
>
> *Keeping me locked from the Promised Land*
>
> *Where I am created to be*
>
> *Flee from me, Compromise*
>
> *I no more accept your disguise*
>
> *Prison of triviality*
>
> *Wrapping me in mediocrity*
>
> *Choking the truth in fears from lies*
>
> *Heavenly freedom, explode*
>
> *Lift me into the dimensions you've told*
>
> *Will unite your eternal breath*
>
> *With mine, as I resurrect from death*
>
> *And the beauty of You unfolds…*
>
> — *Elisabet Leiboelle Fountain*

Christ took back from Satan the authority God had given to Adam. When Christ overcame principalities and powers to sit at the right hand of God, he took back the authority Adam gave to Satan through the Fall. He has delegated it to us as sons of God **(Colossians 2:15; Revelation 12:7-10)**.

Christ gave back what Satan stole from mankind and became our new legal representative in the spirit realm.

When we are born into the Kingdom of God as His children, we receive power of attorney, legal authority on His behalf on the earth.

Colossians 1:13-16 is the message of the new Kingdom where we now reside. As believers we have been transferred from under Satan's authority to under Christ's, into a new "kingdom." Christ's redemption brings us to a place of "completeness," spiritual adequacy, and gives us authority. Christ gives us the ability to live victoriously over and above the invisible powers of darkness. When we live and love as citizens of the heavenly kingdom, this becomes true in the natural realm instead of just theoretically believing it in the spirit realm **(Philippians 3:20)**.

Ephesians 6:12 says *for our struggle is not against flesh and blood, but against the rulers, against the authorities, against the powers of this dark world and against the spiritual forces of evil in the heavenly realms.*

Paul reminds us that we have spiritual authority and blessings in the unseen or *heavenly realms* **(Ephesians 1:3)**. God wants people to be delivered from the power of Satan and his forces **(Ephesians 2:1-9)**.

Examples of when we use spiritual authority:

- When you are having tormenting dreams or thoughts and you say, "In the name of Jesus I command this tormenting spirit to go."

- When you believe something you know isn't really true, but it's how you feel, then you tell those lies to stop attacking your mind in the name of Jesus.

- When praying for your family, you are pro-active on their behalf by taking authority over the enemy's activities in their life.

Discussion:

In what area of your life do you need to apply spiritual authority?

We don't have to fear Satan.

The good news is that Satan and his forces have already been defeated and disarmed (Colossians 2:15). Therefore, there's no need for believers to fear their spiritual enemy. While Satan still has the freedom to tempt and harass Christians, he has no direct authority over them. The armor of God pictures the protection Jesus gives us against demonic attack (Ephesians 6:12-18).

Prayer: Lord, show me any place in my heart where I don't believe my enemies are defeated. I repent for not trusting you to fight my battles. Show me how to pray for the areas where I have trouble trusting and believing your word to be true.

Spiritual warfare for believers, therefore, is fought in the mind, emotions and will. Scriptural truth is our primary line of defense. That's why Paul frequently urges us to be renewed in our minds (Romans 12:1-2; Colossians 3:1-3). The more our minds are filled with the truth of God's Word, the less susceptible we are to Satan's deceptions and temptations. The Word is our sword against the enemy.

However, because Satan still rules the unbelieving world, we will, on occasion, have to confront Satan's work in people's lives as in Acts 13:9-12.

This happens when we get to the root of the problem, the entry point, and expose the lie they believe. For example, a person may be convinced she can't do something based on a lie she believes about herself. When she goes to the first time she began to believe the lie, expose the enemy, and invite Jesus to come into the memory to speak truth. The result is freedom and healing.

When people believe a lie, we can speak the truth to them, but until Jesus comes and speaks to them, they will not believe it.

There is freedom and victory when we worship.

Worship is another path to freedom. Because we are seated at Jesus' right hand, when we worship we ascend to our rightful position. When we abide with Him we can operate in the spiritual authority God has given us. That is why Satan doesn't want us to be free in worship. God called Israel out of Egypt to worship, but Pharaoh didn't want to let them go because he knew that if they were free to worship their God, his own power to control them was over.

When we worship, we are focused on Christ and who He is — the Restorer of our souls.

Because Israel didn't have a new spirit to go with their new life of freedom, they could not believe that God would do something supernatural even though they had seen the miraculous. As Christians, our spirit is made new so we should be tuned in to the Spirit of God. As we worship we become instruments of righteousness. We are to be a symphony of sound (worship) in the earth for His glory.

At salvation, our spirit has come to life and we are each given a new heart.

This new heart gives us a revelation of the love of God and His perfect provision. If we understand sin, the result is a broken and contrite heart.

As we grow in our walk with Christ and renew our minds through the Word of God, we deepen our understanding of sin and the effect it has on our hearts. As our hearts become conformed to His, we are better able to love others as He does, and sin breaks our hearts as it breaks His.

But in order to help others come into wholeness, first we need to be healed and whole ourselves. There is medical proof that chemical poisons are released through the body by toxic emotions such as unforgiveness, bitterness, anger, resentment, fear, anxiety, and frustrations. Not dealing with these issues of the heart can cause disease in the body as well as the soul.

> *Bitterness is like a rock thrown into a placid pond; after its initial splash, it sends out concentric circles that disturb the whole pond. It starts with ourselves, expands to our spouse, then out to our children, friends and colleagues.*
> —Dr. Chuck Lynch, *I Should Forgive, but . . .*

Discussion:

Have you ever known someone who had a physical illness due to emotional stress? Has that ever happened to you?

Final thought:

We live in a new kingdom with a kingdom authority over the powers of darkness.

God Moment:

When your mind is in turmoil and confusion, be still and picture Jesus in the midst of the storm. Ask God to show you any place the enemy has an open door to bring chaos into your life.

Repent and ask God what you need to do next. He knows the plans He has for you … to give you a hope and a future. Hopelessness is not from God; He always gives hope and has a plan. Ask Him to show you what He is doing in the circumstances.

Jeremiah 29:10-11, 31:2-4, 31:16-17, 33:3

Assignment:

Describe a time in your life when you prayed with boldness and as a result saw the enemy defeated?

_____

_____

What are some areas where you are not standing strong against Satan's attack?

_____

_____

What would make you afraid to stand against the powers of darkness on your behalf or on behalf of others?

_____

_____

Lesson 6: Walk in Humility

Have you ever prayed, or heard someone else pray, "Lord, if it be your will, please heal …"? Yet Jesus never prayed to ask the Father to heal someone. He did it himself, and told us to do the same, based on our delegated authority from Him. So we can reasonably conclude that God desires for us to be healed: spirit, soul, and body.

> *Our premise, based on* Matthew 8:2, *and* 9:28, *is that not only is God able to heal, but He also wills to heal.*
> — Karen Cudzilo

The Tabernacle Veil was torn so we can come into the presence of God.

Matthew 27:51 says when Jesus was crucified the veil in the Temple was torn from top to bottom. According to Rabbinic literature, this veil was as thick as a man's hand, 20 feet wide, and 60 feet high. It is also said that a team of oxen tied to either end of the Veil pulling in different directions could not have pulled it apart. Only God could have torn it. He wants a relationship with us, not just mental assent, and without the veil we have legal access directly to Him for that relationship to flourish.

Hebrews 10:20 says the veil represents the flesh, the soul, that is, what we can see, hear and understand in the natural.

Before our spirit is plugged into God's, living from an intellectual worldview can separate us from God. Hebrews 9:23-24 says Jesus took His blood into the original Tabernacle in heaven, and after applying it to the altar, sat down at the right hand of God.

Now that we are saved by the Blood of Christ, if we sin and then repent, there is no longer anything that separates us from God. We have a new identity in Christ; we have become part of the priesthood (1 Peter 2:9). We are clothed in rich robes of righteousness like Joshua in Zechariah 3:4. It's important to realize Satan has no legal right to accuse us to God because we now have a High Priest who went behind the Veil to atone for our sins. He placed His blood on the altar in heaven so now His blood covers our sin, past, present and future. He is our great High Priest who is constantly interceding for us (Hebrews 2:7, 4:14, 7:25).

Since Satan has no more claim on us, he tries to use us against each other in order to cause offenses. He knows that to overcome his strongholds we need each other. So, if he can keep the Body of Christ separated, then his hold in certain areas of a believer's life are less likely to be resolved. Offenses are Satan's bait to open the door to unforgiveness and to give a root of bitterness an opportunity to grow.

Discussion:

How have you seen an offense destroy a family or a friendship?

Jesus said Satan had no place in Him.

Satan was full of pride and wanted to be like God, but Jesus who *was* part of the Godhead humbly and willingly left His position in heaven in order to save us (Philippians 2:5-13).

Satan's sin was pride, so when we live a life of humility, we live a life of victory, giving him no place in us. Sometimes we have to first humble ourselves and admit we have a problem in order to ask someone to pray for us. It is always easier to pray for someone else's problem than to ask them to pray for us (Ezekiel 28:2-17).

Beth Moore, in her book *Praying God's Word,* points out that pride cheats us of contentment, healing, holiness, vision, genuine friendships, and even love, among other things. That's a pretty high price to pay. Don't let Satan use your pride to rob you of so much.

Satan's tactics of deception include temptation to the body, soul and spirit.

2 Corinthians 2:11 reminds us we are not ignorant of Satan's schemes. So be aware of some of his most common tactics:

- *Accusations and suspicion* If you tend to jump to conclusions, stop and check your facts. You rarely have all the facts at once. Then check your assumptions, motives and heart. While your conclusions may be correct, it's just as likely the evil one is trying to stir up trouble. So keep an open mind, and extend grace. 1 Corinthians 12:10 lists many spiritual gifts, but remember there is not a gift of discernment; it's a gift of *discerning of spirits*, which is quite different.

- *Lust of the eyes,* which is clarified in Matthew 5:28 as all desires of the heart, thoughts and esthetic senses, whether followed by actions or not.

- *Lust of the flesh* Also known as the tempter, Satan uses all our bodily appetites against us with seducing spirits and lust to try and turn us away from God (Romans 1:27).

- *Pride of life* anything to make one wise (appeals to the mind in acquiring knowledge and spiritual insight especially through the occult (1 John 2:16). The pride of life is also known as vainglory. This deceptive tactic of Satan's is being overly focused on or proud of one's own achievements, accomplishments or possessions. This is particularly successful in appeals to the mind — to make one wise or more knowledgeable. Promises of special spiritual insight, especially through the occult apply here.

Pride is the deification of self.
— Oswald Chambers, *My Utmost for His Highest*

As a man, Jesus was tempted body, soul, and spirit in the wilderness. Satan offered Jesus kingdoms, power and glory (Matthew 4:1-11). Where Adam gave his authority to the enemy, Jesus resisted the temptation.

God said, "Let us make man in our image." I believe He made him a triune being of body, soul and spirit. The Star of David with its two triangles interlocked can be seen as symbolic of the Messiah who links the tri-unity of God with the tri-unity of man. Perhaps it represents God's triune being reaching down to men and man's triune being reaching up to God.

Satan had no success in enticing Jesus to sin because Jesus was not born with a sin nature.

The Holy Spirit conceived Jesus. When Satan tried to tempt Jesus using his appeals to the usual weaknesses of man: power, pride, etc., he failed, and Jesus was victorious.

When we obey the Word and resist the devil by NOT agreeing with his lies, it brings a greater anointing, or blessing, as we grow in our faith and relationship with God.

Jesus was obedient in His public baptism, identifying for the first time with the sin of mankind; even though He had no personal sin for which to repent, it showed the spirit realm that He was submitting to God's authority.

Let's go back over that again. Watch what Jesus did. First, He set an example with the Word by defeating Satan with the word of God; that is still our strongest weapon today. After He was tempted in the desert, He began His ministry in the power of the Spirit, beginning with an act of obedience. When we overcome temptation, we have more authority in the spirit realm and a stronger anointing or blessing from God.

Satan uses man to gain position and power.

The earth as we know it is a natural realm, and we have physical bodies. Satan and his demons do not have physical bodies, yet they want to have power and control in our natural world. So they accomplish their work through humans when they can control one's thinking and actions.

Satan's realm of influence is the mind and soul, because that is where the decisions of life are made — that is, made and then carried out by the will. For this reason, the body and soul still need cleansing and renewal after salvation (Romans 12:1-2).

Isaiah 45:18 indicates God did not create the earth in vain (*tohu*). The word means a formless chaotic mess, a waste, worthless thing, emptiness and desolation, for no purpose, for nothing. This word first occurs in Genesis 1:2 "the earth was without form (*tohu*) and void (*bohu*). *Tohu* and *bohu* are coupled together to describe a scene of disorder, confusion, and lack of arrangement. In E.W. Bullinger's *Bible Companion*, he says that he believes that the earth was not originally the way we see it described in Genesis 1:2.

Perhaps Satan had a kingdom of some kind on the earth before Adam ever existed; scripture says he was in Eden (Ezekiel 28:13). It appears to be before Adam was ever in the garden. When he approached Adam and Eve in the garden, he was already a fallen being. He had ruled over a kingdom, and in order for him to ascend into heaven as it says in Ezekiel 28, and exalt his throne above the stars of God, means that kingdom could have been here on earth.

So when he fell, along with a third of the angels, the earth became infested with spiritual darkness. Apparently, the spirits here now are the ones who are not held in chains but are part of Satan's rebellion, evil spirits looking for a body through which to express their personality. If they can't embody a human, they will embody an animal, whatever it takes to inhabit a being or express their personality (Luke 10:18-19; Revelation 12:9).

God didn't create Satan and his minions the way they are now.

Scripture says Lucifer was perfect in his way from the day he was created and that he was a leader. Then iniquity was found in him; pride was his downfall. So Satan/Lucifer, the devil, is a fallen angel, probably an archangel (Ezekiel 28:15). This could have happened before the creation of Man.

Some Bible scholars believe that there was some pre-Adamic creation here before man. We saw that in Genesis it says the earth was without form and void describing the condition of earth as a result of judgment (Jeremiah 4:23-26).

In Genesis God told Adam to *replenish* the earth. Some commentators believe 2 Peter 3:1-13 might not be referring to the flood in Noah's day but to an earlier flood. In **verse 6** the word used for world is *cosmos* – it means *the world system*. Some scholars believe that kind of destruction didn't happen in Noah's day.

Psalms 8:5 shows a new order of creation. Before it was the Godhead, Archangels, and then angels. Now it is the

Godhead, man, and then the angelic realm. The word for angels is "*elohim.*" Man was made to rule, but he fell into the deception of thinking he could be his own god and control his destiny.

Satan's five "I wills" of Isaiah 14:12-14**, the original sin of rebellion:**

- I will ascend into heaven — he had to go up from somewhere (earth?) to ascend.

- I will exalt my throne above the stars of God — he had a throne and therefore, a kingdom (on earth?)

- I will sit upon the mount of the congregation, in the sides of the north — this is where God's throne was, so he was after God's place of ruling and reigning.

- I will ascend above the heights of the clouds — many Bible scholars think he was here on earth "the world that then was."

- I will be like the most High — he wanted to be worshiped and be in control.

The result was that he was cast out of heaven (Luke 10:18), which could be what happened to the earth that caused it to become without form and void. If they did have a kingdom on the earth, it became a waste because of judgment against Satan's rebellion. But the spirits remained. We don't know for sure what happened before man was created, but we do know today that we are tempted in the same ways by those five "I wills."

Those "I wills" influence mankind.

As humans in a fallen world, we seem to have an overwhelming, innate desire for self will, pleasure, and power.

- **Self-will** - is the essence of "I'll do it myself," wanting to be in control, having what we want when we want it, and usually without realizing it, being controlled by personal ambition.

- **Pleasure** - in moderation is a gift from God, but uncontrolled, it is license to indulge in every appetite: sex, food, lust, possessions, etc.

- **Power** - too often sits on throne of the heart of Man. In a fallen world, man wants to be his own god and determine his own destiny, by any means possible: through the occult, humanism, scientific intellectualism, and assumed equality with God. These misappropriated wrong motives give power to Satan when it becomes more about us than others, and about being in control.

In our celebrity-riddled culture, we want the worship from men that only God should receive. If Satan can get us to willfully sin using any of these areas of weakness, he has a legal right to enter our lives. The key is our will and our freedom to choose.

But don't be discouraged when you find yourself falling short of God's standard. We don't have to be perfect for God to use us, or to be confident in exercising spiritual authority over the enemy. We have the power of Jesus through repentance and forgiveness, so with God, all things are possible.

Final thought:

God has given us all we need to live victoriously.

God Moment:

Imagine yourself standing before God. Now tell Him all the things that you fear. Tell Him where you feel most defeated and what you are struggling with. See Him placing armor on you to battle those things.

Ask Him what is true and what is your part in it all. Now as you stand in His Truth watch - because all you have to do is claim His truths and stand next to Him as He fights your battle.

1 Timothy 1:19; 1 Samuel 17:47; 1 Chronicles 5:20

Assignment:

If you know you have been brought out of darkness and translated into the Kingdom of Light, how do you walk that out daily?

_____

_____

What is the giant in your life that you are facing that threatens your peace and spiritual victory in ruling over your circumstances?

_____

_____

Where is the spirit of pride ruling your life, rather than a spirit of humility?

_____

_____

Make a list of anything you think the Lord has shown you that you need to deal with – the trash in your life that needs taking out.

_____

_____

Lesson 7: Walk in Authority

Success — as God Sees It.

In order to exercise spiritual authority and have influence in the spirit realm, we need to give God control of our lives. By giving Him control, He can bring us into our destiny in Him. We will be confident He has given us a place of influence and spiritual authority through His favor. The result is the joy that comes from serving others, not controlling others.

Jesus gave us back the dominion and authority that Adam willfully gave away, but we have to actively cooperate with the Holy Spirit to realize it. That means having our will in tune with God's will, through the Holy Spirit who indwells our spirit. We are successful when we begin to act on the little we know to do. God will honor our efforts.

Before promotion there will always be temptation.

Jesus' ministry began after he resisted Satan. Overcoming temptation gives us an "upgrade" in the spirit realm. As you study the Bible, you'll rarely see God's calling revealed in a person's life without being preceded by testing, training or temptation. But God honors our victories. When you overcome the temptation, you receive a greater anointing (that is, effectiveness, revelation or blessing).

The Holy Spirit energizes and works through the soul, spirit and body in cooperation with the will of man (Philippians 2:13-17). Spiritual authority increases as you submit to Christ and gain personal victories because your confidence grows. If an unholy spirit has control, it will work through the powers of the soul and members of the body, if their will has given it the power to be in control.

Discussion:

In what ways do we give the enemy control?

We break the enemy's hold on us by destroying any legal openings he has into our lives. We repent of wrong patterns of thinking and beliefs we have about whatever was associated with the door we opened to the enemy. We surrender them to Jesus and submit ourselves completely to God's power to deliver us. When we do this, we loose negative influences of the world from our lives.

Have you noticed how when garbage is left on the streets, it attracts rats? Get rid of the garbage, and the rats will leave too. The same is true in our spiritual lives. If you notice spiritual rats, look more closely and find the garbage attracting them.

When spiritually battling for our minds, victory starts with us.

It's the garbage that attracts the rats. What opened the door to the enemy to gain entry into our lives? It could be the strongholds, sin, soul ties, vows, word curses, or otherwise coming into agreement (knowingly or not) with the enemy.

Clean your house, spiritually speaking. Break apart the effects of the work of the enemy in every area of life: finances, family, home, and work.

Prayer: Father, I repent for the sin and wrong attitudes that have opened a door to the enemy. I ask for forgiveness and cleansing. I speak to every spirit of darkness that has attached itself to my mind and command it to leave in the name of Jesus. Thank you Lord. Amen.

Jesus is seated at the right hand of the Father, which is a place of authority. History tells us that to sit at the right of someone in power means to sit in a place of favor and authority. We died with Christ and we are raised in Christ, seated with Him in the heavens (Ephesians 1:17-23, 2:1-10).

1 Corinthians 6:17 says if we are joined to the Lord, then we are one spirit with Him. If we are spiritually seated in the heavens in Christ Jesus and all things have been put under His feet, along with ours, why are we living like helpless, vulnerable paupers? It's because we don't practice a resurrection gospel. We don't believe we have been raised with Christ. We still see Him on the cross and ourselves there with Him, feeling oppressed and defeated. We've forgotten the rest of the story: that we, with Christ, have been raised in resurrection power to live a victorious life.

When Jesus rose from the grave, scripture says He triumphed over Satan in the fact that He had conquered death. Satan had done all he could do to defeat Jesus, but Jesus won, and reigns. The cross is significant, but so is the empty tomb — even more so. It means we, too, have been empowered to reign over the enemy, and that's what happens when we resist the temptation of the devil and draw near to God (James 4:7).

Galatians 2:20 says we are crucified with Christ. We are no longer living our own lives, because Jesus is living in us. We have been resurrected into a completely new way of living. He has made us victorious with Him over the demonic realm, and that victory is our reality whether we experience it or not.

This new way of living enables us to have victory over the enemy in all areas: renewing our minds, healing, deliverance, etc. In other words, we are able to be proactive against the enemy.

Hebrews 10:12-13 says Jesus is seated at the right hand of God waiting for His enemies to be made a footstool. We are called to take part in that, but we have to understand it's supernatural. It should come naturally to us when by faith, we know it's already accomplished in the supernatural. It will be true in the natural when we really believe we have authority over the enemy, and are willing to step out in faith and act on that belief.

It would be accurate to say that the right hand of God is the center of power of the whole universe. We need a revelation that we are seated right there with Christ at God's right hand, above all these powers we have to deal with. Jesus is the head, and we are His body. The head needs the body to accomplish what the head wants to do on the earth. We are told to exercise authority over the devil, not wait on Jesus to do it for us. He has already accomplished all He needs to do for us to win the battle. Now it's up to us to be bold in our stand. Only the Holy Spirit can impart that kind of boldness.

The enemy knows that if the Church ever gets a true revelation of the Holy Spirit's role, he will be in trouble.

Hebrews 1:13 says He didn't say to the angels to sit at His right hand; He gave us that honor. In **Jude** the Archangel didn't rebuke Satan over the body of Moses because he had no authority. Perhaps Moses gave Satan the legal right to demand his body when he murdered the Egyptian, or later when he was disobedient to God's instructions about speaking to the rock **(Numbers 20:8-12)**.

The transference of the believer from under Satan's authority to Christ's authority is described as movement from one kingdom into another.

Colossians 1:13 says He has delivered us from the power or authority of darkness and translated us into the kingdom of His dear Son. So this means Satan has no right to mess with us unless we give it to him. Ensuing verses describe Christ's redemption as bringing us to a place of "completeness" — this is, of spiritual adequacy, authority, or ability to live victoriously over and above the invisible powers of darkness (Colossians 1:14-20; 2:6-10).

This becomes functionally true, as opposed to merely theoretically true, when we:

- **Live** and love as citizens of the heavenly kingdom (Philippians 3:20).

- **Utilize** this kingdom's currency, which is of irresistible and immeasurable value (Acts 3:6).

- **Operate** as ambassadors authorized to offer kingdom peace and reconciliation to those not yet renewed in Christ (2 Corinthians 5:20).

- **Serve** as the kingdom militia, girded for prayerful conflict against the dark powers controlling so much of this present world (Ephesians 6:10-20).

This is the practical application to all our living. It is how to live a supernatural life naturally.

Matthew 28:18-20 says all power and authority has been given to Jesus and He has delegated it to the Church (Mark 16:15-18).

The word authority (*exousia*) implies the right to exercise a given power. It means *delegated responsibility*. I read an example of a policeman stopping traffic. He has only to hold his hand up in the air and we stop. That is because we recognize the governmental power that backs up his authority. In Luke 10:19 the word for power is actually authority.

We represent the Kingdom of God and He has given us authority over the enemy. God backs us up in the spirit realm. Our authority is delegated authority. We ask God to stop the enemy but He has told us to do it under his delegated authority (Mark 16:17-18). When the Holy Spirit imparts boldness, we have confidence in approaching God. We stand against the enemy in our delegated authority in Jesus' name (1 John 5:14).

A policeman doesn't have to be strong enough to physically stop the traffic because he knows there is a power that backs up his authority. Jesus has both power and authority. *What He delegates to us is the authority to call for His power.* When we come against the enemy, it isn't based on our strength; that comes from Jesus. He is the power that backs up our authority. Ephesians 6:10 says to be strong in the Lord; it's in the power of His might. The centurion in Luke 7:2-10 was a heathen soldier, but he understood the nature of earthly authority and realized heavenly authority would work the same way. Jesus acknowledged his faith, so we, too, should pay attention to the parallels between heavenly and earthly authority.

Jesus has the keys of hell and of death.

After he stripped the demonic powers of authority that had been theirs since the Fall, Christ made a show of them openly, triumphing over them. (Revelation 1:18; Colossians 2:15). Now with the keys of authority, Jesus is seated above those powers at the right hand of His Father, and rules from the throne of God through his Body the Church.

Matthew 18:18 says that whatever we bind on earth is bound in heaven. That is what happens when we are exercising spiritual authority. When we pray, something happens in the unseen realm of the spirit. This is the kingdom of God advancing.

However, when we hold onto unforgiveness it prevents or binds heaven from moving on our behalf. If we want to exercise authority over the darkness, our hearts must be right before God. It does not mean we have to be perfect. Even if we don't have it all together, it doesn't change the fact that we are all washed in the Blood of righteousness before God.

God looks at your heart and motive.

Empowered by the Spirit.

We see in Matthew 3:14 that John the Baptist did not want to baptize Jesus because he knew Jesus was sinless. After all, we are baptized to signify our forgiveness, but Jesus had nothing to be forgiven for. He had been conceived by the Holy Spirit, and had never sinned. So we see that this was Jesus' first public association with the sin of mankind.

The Holy Spirit came as the Father expressed His pleasure in the Son because of His obedience in submitting to a baptism of repentance even though He had no sin (Matthew 3:17).

At His baptism, Jesus received the anointing of the Holy Spirit to begin His ministry. We have no record of Him performing miracles before this time. He had already overcome Satan in the wilderness three times, but this is when He became an active threat to Satan and his kingdom. Because Jesus lives in us as believers, we, too, are threats to Satan. We can't defeat him with our own power or by ourselves, but with Christ, all things are possible. That is why it is so important for us to be empowered by the Holy Spirit (Matthew 3:16).

The Spirit conceived Jesus, but He still needed to be empowered by the Spirit. So how much more do we need that same anointing that the 120 received on the Day of Pentecost in the upper room? They were believers, but they needed the baptism of the Holy Spirit's fire. Ask Jesus to do that for you and ask Him to baptize you with the Holy Spirit. You receive the Holy Spirit at the new birth, but I believe there is an empowerment needed in order to do the works that Jesus did. Just as Jesus was born of the Spirit, so are we, and like Jesus, we have to be empowered for ministry.

Prayer: Lord Jesus, I repent of any occult involvement in my life no matter how innocent it seems to me or to the world. (This might be playing with Ouija boards, séances, having your palm read, reading your horoscopes, tarot cards, going to a fortune teller or psychic, etc.) I ask you now to forgive me and to baptize me in your Holy Spirit. Thank you Lord. Amen.

He breathed on them in John 20:22 and told them to receive the Holy Spirit. Were they born again at that time? The same word for breathed is also used in Genesis 2:7 at creation. Was the upper room experience their new birth or an empowerment to fulfill their calling?

Discussion:

Do you think the disciples were born again when Jesus breathed on them in John 20:22? In what way did the disciples' lives change after the tongues of fire came down on them?

If a spiritual language is part of the package *be willing to be willing* to accept it. We need all the building up we can get **(1 Corinthians 14:4; Jude 20)**. Know that if you begin to pray in a new language, Satan will try to make you doubt that anything has really happened to you. If you ask, you receive, even though you might not speak in a different language at the time, because we don't all have the same experience.

The important thing is to ask for the empowerment of the Spirit to do the work of the ministry — whatever that looks like for you.

Right after receiving the Holy Spirit and hearing God speak, Satan tried to put doubt in Jesus' mind by saying, "**if** you are the Son of God" **(Matthew 4:3)**. He did this to try and prevent Jesus from fulfilling His calling and destiny. If Jesus had given in to Satan's lies, it seems that Satan would have ruled not only the earth but also Jesus and the entire heavenly realm.

Satan will try to do the same to you. He will try to make you doubt God's word and even your salvation. He will cause you to doubt your anointing for ministry. He wants you to think it's your own dreams, not the destiny God has called you to fulfill.

God Moment:

"Beloved, I have equipped you to battle the enemy. Now as you stand before me, allow me to anoint your mind to understand your spiritual authority and what that should look like in your life.

"If you believe some of your armor is missing, ask Me to open your eyes to the truth concerning your weapons. I have already given you everything you need, so ask Me to help you see what you have that you are not using against the enemy."

Now picture God taking those weapons out of the closet and cleaning them up for you and handing each one to you.

Thank Him for all He has given you and ask forgiveness for any doubt you have concerning His ability to win your battles through you.

1 Samuel 17:47; 2 Samuel 22:40; Psalms 18:39

Assignment:

When have you used scripture as an effective weapon against the enemy?

_____

_____

Have you been effectively using the weapons God has given you?

_____

_____

In what area do you feel unequipped to stand up against the enemy?

_____

_____

Why do you think that is a problem area for you?

_____

_____

Final thought:

When we don't feel equipped to do battle against the enemy in certain areas the Lord will give us the confidence we need.

Lesson 8: Walk in Victory

In the spirit realm, there are two domains or kingdoms.

Spiritually speaking, Satan's domain or kingdom operates from what is referred to as the second heaven, an invisible realm. In Colossians 1:12-16 the Greek word for domain is *excusia* which means power of authority. The second heaven is where Satan exercises his authority over the earth. You'll recall that this right to rule over the earth was given to him by Adam. Spiritual attacks against us come not from God but from this invisible realm where Satan rules.

The third heaven is God's dwelling. The word in 2 Chronicles 2:6 for heaven is *shamayim* and the *im* is plural meaning more than one heaven. The Hebrew meaning is the highest heavens or a third heaven which implies more than one. This is God's domain where Paul, in 2 Corinthians 12:2, had his experience with God.

It is from the second heaven that Satan contests God's will for man, and his hierarchy of principalities and powers gain legal right to block heaven's will through our rebellion and willful sin (Ephesians 2:2). However, we have the authority to do warfare against Satan and his schemes, to break through those powers, and restore God's will for our lives.

Satan's Kingdom of spiritual darkness operates against us in three levels:

- Private/personal
- Communal/familial
- Territorial/geographical

Discussion:

How do these areas of spiritual darkness affect us?

Man was created to have fellowship with God who is Spirit.

There is a spiritual void in us that causes us to gravitate toward the supernatural. Man was created to have fellowship with God who is Spirit; therefore a relationship to the supernatural is "natural" for man. If we don't know the true supernatural power of God we will be in danger of being deceived by the supernatural power of the enemy (2 Corinthians 11:3).

Prayer: Father, thank you that John 16:13 says your Holy Spirit guides me into all truth. Holy Spirit, search my heart and show me any areas of deception in my life, help me to discern truth. Please help me to hear your voice and not be deceived by the enemy. Please give me wisdom, discernment, and understanding (Proverbs 2:6).

People become deceived when they look to the wrong source for supernatural power and manifestations. It leads them to get involved in occult practices like mind control, reading tarot cards, psychics, spirit guides, fortune telling, channeling, astrology, wizardry, witchcraft, spiritualism, talking to the dead, etc.

God says these things are an abomination to Him and are forbidden practices (Leviticus 18:21-25,19:31, 20:6). He wants to protect people from spiritual deception and demonic influence. Most people would not participate in these practices if they realized that all of these are Satanic and that merely by participating, they are actually worshiping Satan.

When people think they are communicating with dead loved ones, it is actually familiar or familial spirits masquerading as their loved ones.

Example:

I once was asked by church leaders to pick up a girl from the airport who had flown in from Ohio for the day for prayer. She had read a book about the Holy Spirit that our pastor at that time had written. She was seeking more of the Holy Spirit in her life. Another lady and I picked her up, took her to lunch, and brought her to the church for prayer. While driving back, I looked in the rear view mirror at her while she was speaking, and I saw two big slanted eyes with slits looking back at me. I was startled and thought, What is this??

When we prayed with her, there seemed to be something blocking her from receiving more of the Holy Spirit. I asked her if she had ever been involved in the occult in any way. She said no, so I asked her if she had been involved in any séances or ever communicated with the dead. She said that oh yes, her deceased grandmother came most nights to talk with her. She would awaken her in the middle of the night to visit. All she saw were her eyes. I told her it was a demonic "familial" or familiar spirit masquerading as her grandmother. The Holy Spirit caused me to see the demonic spirit behind the deception, and I was able to tell her what I saw.

Christians can be susceptible to being deceived this way because they miss the person who had an impact on their life. Perhaps they felt loved and accepted by this person while feeling rejected by other family members.

Those spirits that manifest and claim to be someone you know are actually familiar spirits who know about the past since demons exist and have existed throughout history. They need a body to inhabit and express themselves, so they deceive people into believing the lie that the person has lived before. They know the events of history because they were on the earth, so they are familiar with the times and the family history.

Discussion:

Have you ever dabbled in any of the above things, innocently or otherwise? If the answer is yes, stop now, repent, and ask the Lord to forgive you.

Prayer: *Father, in the name of Jesus I renounce all occult involvement and I repent for my actions. I close the door to the enemy and command all evil spirits who gained entry into my life through these activities to leave in the name of Jesus. Amen*

People are drawn into the occult for different reasons.

Some people are drawn in because they want to be loved; others want position and power. Some want to overcome personal limitations while others want their life to have meaning, and others want community – a place where they feel they fit in. There are those who want personal growth, and think this may be a way to learn, and still others like the experience of reaching a spiritual high. However, all are wrong. If you've been drawn in or deceived, God offers us forgiveness and mercy. Repent today, using the prayer outlined above.

Regardless of any seemingly right motives or needs in searching for more in life, the people who get involved in the occult are deceived. Satan will try to take over their lives if they let him. At first he will stay in the background, but the deeper they get involved, the more demonic it becomes. Just look at our entertainment industry over time. As movies have progressed technologically, they have regressed morally, spiritually and emotionally under the guise of "amusement."

One particularly insidious strategy Satan has with young people is games on the Internet. He uses them to gain entry into a person's mind. Kids and adults are just playing games, but Satan is using some of these innocent looking activities to draw them into more serious occult practices. If you're sensitive to such influences, the artwork alone is enough to give you pause. It is not innocent, and sets you up by de-sensitizing you to violence, illicit sex, and perversion.

> *Sin wears a cloak of deception. Therefore, the first stage . . . involves the exposure of our hearts to truth and the cleansing of our hearts from lies. Once the Spirit breaks the power of deception in our lives, He can break the power of sin.*
> — Francis Frangipane, *Holiness, Truth and the Presence of God*

The good news is that no matter how enmeshed someone is in the occult they can be set free.

Jesus defeated Satan in the wilderness, was tempted and resisted him on our behalf as well as His own. If Jesus had given in to his temptation He would've gained world power but would have also been bowing down to Satan, and as a result so would we. Jesus would have been second in command, and we would have had no power over Satan.

Assuming Satan was prepared to keep his promise to give Jesus the world, (remember, he is the father of lies and deception), it would have been worth it to him to give up his earthly domain if he could have gained power over the Godhead and achieved the worship he wanted from heaven and earth. His goal has always been to exalt his throne above God's and to be worshiped by men and angels.

Being tempted is not a sin; it's the yielding to the temptation that results in sin. Hebrews 2:18 says Jesus can aid man because He, too, was tempted.

When Jesus went to the cross He defeated Satan on our behalf.

Colossians 1:19-20 says all things on earth and in heaven were reconciled to Himself by Him, having made peace by the blood of His cross. In other words He put things right, the way they were intended to be in the first place. He took His blood into heaven and cleansed the altar in heaven where the original Most Holy Place is located (Hebrews 9:12, 23-24).

This placement of the blood also represents cleansing the altar of your heart. That gives us access and the legal right to be seated with Him figuratively, and one day literally, because we have the right to enter heaven itself. Verse 21 says we are presented holy and blameless if we don't move away from the gospel. He redeemed us, which means He bought us back — transported us out of the kingdom of darkness into the kingdom of light.

There is a strong pull from the spirit realm today to move us away from the gospel. Scripture says that, "in that day, if possible, even the elect would be deceived" (Matthew 24:24). In the world today a big deception is to believe that any doorway and any path will get you to heaven. There is also a lie that all gods being worshiped in other religions are the same as the God of the Bible. I have to believe that the "that day" Jesus spoke of is here.

Our young people have been targeted through the media with romantic vampire novels, young people killing each other to survive, and charming characters like Harry Potter teaching them witchcraft. And next came a "romance" series on bondage. Remember that words have power. It puts a new perspective on headlines describing one of the New York Times best-selling books: "*Fifty Shades of Gray* kinky romance is a hot hit … sexy or sick?" It was called "mommy porn." The guy in the story is a rich billionaire who enjoys domination and bondage. *And this is a love story??* No, it is a seduction of our minds as Satan tries to come in the side door, dulling our senses so we will accept the next thing and ultimately, to bring us into bondage. In the meantime, 1 Peter 5:8 says Satan our adversary walks about seeking to destroy. When we resist and draw near to God, he will flee.

God has delivered us from the power of darkness.

Colossians 2:15 indicates that wicked spirits in Ephesians 6:12 are fallen angels. Jesus has dethroned them so we can have authority over them in this life; we don't have to wait until we get to heaven to be free. Colossians 1:12-13 says God has delivered us from the power of darkness and transported us into the Kingdom of His dear Son. That means Satan has no right to rule us.

Luke 10:19 is a truth that will set us free. In Matthew 28:18 Jesus says all power has been given Him in heaven and earth. He delegates that power to us to use against the enemy because we are the Body of Christ on the earth.

In John 14:13-14, Jesus says whatever we ask in His name He will do. The Greek word for asks means *demand*.

That is a far cry from begging Him to do something. When you demand something, it's because you know it is your right and privilege to have it. That is why it's important to understand your authority in spiritual warfare. (**John 16:23-24** is talking about through prayer.) *Our authority is over the spiritual realm, which affects the natural realm, but it's not authority or power over people.*

As believers we are called to a different kind of war.

David's life in battle is a picture of our spiritual warfare. He trained as a shepherd boy, slaying lions and bears to protect his sheep. He was well prepared to slay the giant. He was also tested in his attitude and obedience toward King Saul. He honored Saul's position of authority as ordained by God, even though Saul, the man, did not warrant respect.

Remember that temptation will always come before promotion.

When David was about to battle Goliath, Saul tried to give him his armor, but David was wise enough to say no and not depend on someone else's equipping. We have to fight the enemy with the weapons God has given to us personally. His equipping is custom tailored for each of us. David was confident his weapons worked because he'd already experienced victory when protecting his father's sheep.

We are ready for the bigger battles when we have tested our weapons and armor by winning the smaller ones. Just because someone else does something a certain way and it works for them doesn't mean that's how we should do it. We have to hear from God for ourselves.

Begin exercising spiritual authority and doing warfare with the small things; then you will be ready for the bigger battles. David's early battles were to protect his earthly father's sheep; the battle with Goliath was to protect his heavenly Father's sheep. He saw that the enemy was really challenging the power of God, and it stirred a righteous anger in him. Moreover, he knew exactly how to handle it with perfect confidence that God would give him victory.

David knew he was anointed to be king and that he could do a better job than Saul, but he humbled himself, submitted to Saul's authority, and waited on God's timing for his destiny. That showed a lot of maturity for such a young man. David represents the spiritual man, and Saul represents the carnal or natural man. Likewise, since we are spiritual beings in natural bodies, we need to be aware that we rely on the Holy Spirit for our anointing, and like David, we fight from a place of victory.

In spiritual warfare, it is important to wait on God's timing and to resist the enemy while you are waiting. Part of the process is learning to endure until the end by standing on the Word. Ask yourself what God says about it, or what has He said?

Later God used Saul's attacks on David to test him in his obedience. It was a refining of David's trust in God to bring about what He had promised versus trying to make it happen for himself. When you get a word from God about something, the enemy will try to circumvent it. Abraham and Sarah tried to "help" God along when Ishmael was conceived (Genesis 16:3). That conflict is still happening today. David got it right. The lesson is to wait and trust in God. Follow the adage to be a warrior not a worrier.

Timothy had received prophecies concerning his life and ministry, but he was told that they might not automatically happen without some warfare. 1 Timothy 1:18 says *This charge I commit to you, son Timothy, according to the prophecies previously made concerning you, that by them you may wage the good warfare* — in other words, pray for the fulfillment of the prophecies he'd been given.

Discussion:

What prophesies or promises have you been given? Have you fought for them? Share your experience with your group, or in your journal.

God Moment:

Be still and visit with the Lord; expect Him to speak to you. Be sure to journal what you believe He is saying.

The Lord is inviting you behind the curtain to visit with Him in the Presence of His glory. He wants you to know that it is okay to admit the pain and weariness in your soul. He wants to encourage you in your times of weakness. He is not disappointed in you if you admit your lack of faith or confusion about things around you. When you admit your weakness His strength will be made perfect.

Stop trying to figure things out on your own. You do not have to always be strong. Pour out your heart and listen as He responds. He wants to flood your soul with the peace that only He can give.

"Come my child and receive my blanket of peace. Trust Me."

Hebrews 6:17-19; 2 Corinthians 12:9-10

Assignment:

How would you go about using the weapons God has provided?

_____

_____

When have you actively put on this armor and battled the enemy?

_____

_____

What was the result?

_____

_____

Final thought:

Our battle isn't natural, but supernatural, and we are more than conquerors (Romans 8:37).

Lesson 9: Walk in Love

We have been enlisted in the army of God as citizens of another country.

In Jesus' day the Roman army did more than conquer; they also were to maintain peace in the conquered land, among the conquered people. They implemented the new Roman law in the land and had to be prepared to keep the former rulers and citizens of the country from trying to regain control. Roman soldiers had another important job. They were expected to spread the Roman culture and generally to "Romanize" the part of the world to which they were assigned. When a soldier enrolled in the Roman army, he was immediately granted citizenship, or it was granted to him after his term of service. When he retired from serving, he was given a grant of land many miles from home.

We have been enlisted in the army of God, and are citizens of His Kingdom. We need to be able to take possession of the (figurative) "land" we've been given. We have to conquer or drive out whatever cultural or spiritual entities that want to rule us and make sure that we rule over them instead. Paul called Timothy a soldier in 2 Timothy 2:3-4, and so are we.

We have been given a different kind of armor for a different kind of war. God's way provides spiritual truths, revealing the supernatural and natural realm. Our battle isn't in the natural but in the supernatural realm as soldiers in the new kingdom, we are fighting in order to take possession (Ephesians 6:12).

Discussion:

What is your understanding about these two realms?

Our weapons are not carnal but supernatural

(2 Corinthians 10:3-5; Ephesians 6:10-18).

Spiritually speaking, the enemy has a very highly structured and well-organized kingdom with descending orders of authority and different rulers and sub-rulers responsible for different areas of their territory. Satan wants to dominate the human race, so the warfare is global. In the natural realm, we operate in a world where Satan is god. But God is God in the spirit world, and that is where we have been delegated the authority of Jesus (Matthew 28:18).

Mark 16:15-18 outlines the extent of our authority and James 4:7 reminds us not to let the devil have any place in our lives.

God is working on our behalf even when it seems He doesn't hear our prayers.

In Daniel 10:2-13 we see the prince was over the kingdom of Persia and apparently under him were lesser angels or kings. Then Michael came to help withstand the enemy (Daniel 12:1). Michael is the archangel who stands guard over Israel. Great prince refers to archangel. The princes of darkness are still ruling over countries and people groups today, and there is a battle in the spirit realm, whether we are aware of it or not.

The four kingdoms that dominated Israel were Babylon (Iraq), Persia (Iran), Greece, and Rome. Persia and Greece were the two dominant Gentile empires at the time. There still is and always will be intense warfare over Israel and Jerusalem in the natural realm, and likewise until Christ's return Christians will always be at war in the supernatural realm.

God has equipped us to defeat the enemy.

To have victory over the enemy we need to have our armor in place and know how to use the weapons God has equipped us with. They are supernatural and used mostly through prayer **(2 Corinthians 10:3-5; Ephesians 6:10-18)**.

The belt (or girdle) of truth represents a clear understanding of God's word. The girdle was a loose tunic-like garment that came to the knees much like Middle Eastern men wear today. It had to be taken care of when they went into action. Like a soldier's belt, it held the rest of the armor in place. When a Roman legionnaire went into battle, he would gather it up, wrapping it more tightly around his body and tucking it into his belt, so it wouldn't hinder his movement.

In order for us to go forward in God, we have to wrap ourselves with truth and bind up those things that will get in the way or hold us back. The enemy doesn't want us to walk in truth because he knows we will experience freedom that will bring victory. Truth means daily living a life of honesty, sincerity, and right motives. Put away hypocrisy, religious clichés, and saying things you don't mean (oaths) **(Matthew 5:37)**.

For an example of a heart issue hindering you, one of my students shared about an older woman who attended another Bible study she was in at the time. The woman came in and sat near her even though she was clearly sick and quite likely contagious at the time. The woman ended up sitting beside her twice. My student was angry with the woman for coming, and she declared the blood of Jesus over herself so she wouldn't get sick too. Rather than being protected against catching the woman's illness, the next day my student woke with a horrible sore throat and feeling sick. The Lord began to speak to her about the woman, who was a widow and really needed to be there. He also showed my student that because of her own resentment, anger, and unforgiveness toward the woman, she had opened herself up to sickness instead of being protected from it. As she realized that her motives were wrong and her heart wasn't right toward the older woman, she confessed to the Lord that her heart wasn't in the right place, repented, and forgave the woman. Immediately, her sore throat went away completely. (Not all sickness is because of these reasons, but it can be, so check your heart whenever you find yourself feeling sick, and make sure you're aligned with God's truth. He may be trying to tell you something.)

The breastplate of righteousness involves guarding your heart.

As the name implies, the breastplate was worn over the heart. Proverbs 4:23 indicates that we should guard our heart with all our strength, because all the things there are in life come out of it. Righteousness involves obedience to the word of God. 1 Thessalonians 5:8 talks about the breastplate of faith and love. This doesn't come from a religious works mentality developed in the mind, but from a heart of faith. It is the righteousness of Christ imparted in grace by the Spirit. When we come to a crisis of belief, it is important that this be in place. (And all of us will experience a crisis of faith at some point).

Discussion:

Have you ever experienced a crisis of belief?

Prayer: *Lord, show me if I have any mindset that involves wrong thinking connected to religious works. I repent of living as if I am still under the law and not under grace. Please speak truth to me. Amen.*

See **Luke 22:31-32** when Jesus prayed for Peter, He prayed that his faith would not fail. Love protects us from the negative forces the enemy wants to establish as strongholds in our minds such as doubt, resentment, unforgiveness, bitterness, depression, hopelessness, unworthiness, etc.

The High Priest wore a breastplate with twelve stones on it representing the twelve tribes of Israel. The High Priest was a mediator between the people and God; wearing the stones over his heart was a reminder to pray for them.

We can learn from this today. **1 Peter 2:19** calls us a royal priesthood, so we can reasonably conclude that just as High Priests in the Old Testament were called to go before God on behalf of the people, we, too, are called to mediate and do warfare prayer on behalf of others – in particular our family, those we carry close to our heart.

The shoes of the preparation of the gospel of peace are our foundation (Ephesians 6:15).

The shoes of the preparation of the gospel of peace mean we are to be prepared to share the gospel. Some Bible translations use the word readiness for preparation. We are to be ready, prepared and willing to share the gospel. The sandals worn in biblical times were made from very strong leather that laced all the way up the calf. The soles were studded with hobnails for sure footing. What a perfect metaphor to illustrate that Jesus with His gospel message is our sure foundation. Everything we are and do is based on the work of the cross and his resurrection power that resides in us.

You must have peace to impart peace.

The shield of faith is big enough to cover the entire body.

In the Roman Empire shields were quite large, rectangular in design and protected the body completely. The darts used in ancient warfare were hollow reeds filled with combustible material. They were set on fire and then shot from bows. If the attacking enemy could not penetrate the wall, they could shoot flaming darts or arrows like miniature missiles over the walls, to set fire to the highly flammable thatched roofs of the houses within the walls. These shields used by the soldiers protected them personally from these flaming missiles.

For us today the shield of faith represents protection under the blood of Christ Jesus. No enemy can penetrate it if the shield of faith has been put in place. Roman shields were made of several thicknesses of bull hide that were stretched over a frame of wood and sometimes strengthened and ornamented with metal rims and pieces of metal. They were rubbed with oil to prevent the leather from drying out and cracking, and to prevent the metal from rusting. When they went into battle, this oiling was especially necessary; "anointing" the shield, that is, rubbing it with oil, was a part of their preparation for war. Today we understand that oil is a symbol of the Holy Spirit.

We oil our shield of faith by asking the Holy Spirit to anoint us for the task at hand.

Faith is the key to hold the shield (protection) in place. I saw a movie battle scene in which warriors banded together in a circle, and those in the middle held their shields over their head while the ones on the outside held theirs in front of them thereby keeping the enemy from penetrating the circle. This is what happens when we intercede on behalf of others. In a similar fashion, you can ask God to protect your heart, health, finances and family and ask other believers to stand with you while resisting the enemy.

Discussion:

How are we vulnerable to the enemy if our shield of faith is not in place?

The helmet of salvation protects our minds.

Satan's primary battlefield is in the mind. He wants to gain entrance to our lives through our thoughts. He was successful when he put the thought into Judas' mind to betray Jesus (John 13:2). Judas had a choice, but God knew what he would choose so He used it to accomplish His purposes.

Satan has no legal right to control our thinking unless we come into agreement with him and open the door to him by believing a lie. We always have a choice about how we respond to thoughts, circumstances and people. We need to always discern where our thoughts are originating. What is the fruit? How does it make you feel? Does it bring peace?

1 Thessalonians 5:8 says our helmet is our hope of salvation. Protection for the heart is faith, but protection for the head is hope. We need both, as they are inextricably related. Hebrews 11:1 tells us that faith is where hope is built.

Hope is a steady expectation of good based on God's Word. It's the attitude that gives us altitude and leaves no room for doubt and self-pity. Hope is a basic part of our salvation experience (Colossians 1:27; Romans 8:24; Hebrews 6:17-20; Ephesians 2:12).

The head of something speaks of having authority while a covered head speaks of submission and protection. A spiritual head wound can affect the whole body — causing depression, doubt, self-pity, suspicion, etc. But hope will not allow those things to control our minds.

The Sword of the Spirit, which is called the Word of God, is the only offensive piece of armor.

The sword of the Spirit is the most powerful piece of armor because that is what Jesus used to defeat Satan in the wilderness. It is an active weapon **(Isaiah 55:10-11)**. **Hebrews 4:12-13** says that it penetrates to every area of the human personality dividing between the soul and spirit.

The word is working to separate our selfish desires, inhibitions, wrong motives and wounds. The Word cleanses the window of our conscience, the meeting place of soul and spirit. It gives us light to see through our own personality and shortcomings and see the best that God has to offer us. It allows us to see into eternity, and it produces faith. It divides between *self* and *spirit*.

My student's experience is an example of the division of soul and spirit. Faith works along this dividing line. We must choose faith over mistrust **(Psalms 37:3, Proverbs 3:5)**. We must discern motives and choose whether to believe God or not, and make daily choices between belief and unbelief **(Hebrews 3:12)**.

The word for spirit is *"rhema,"* which refers to the spoken word. **Revelation 1:16** says Jesus has a double-edged sword coming out of his mouth — the Word. He defeated Satan with the Word of God. You can do the same. When you are going through trials, find a scripture that applies to your situation and actually speak it out loud. The Holy Spirit will keep it from returning void, and it will accomplish its purpose for which it was sent **(Isaiah 55:10-11)**.

It is Christ in us not brute force that wins the battle. His character is our hope of glory and victory over the enemy (Colossians 1:27).

Discussion:

When have you seen the Holy Spirit change a situation after you have stood on scripture to claim your victory? What happened?

God Moment:

The Lord wants you to come and stand before Him and let Him clothe you with new garments. What you are wearing still has the stains of your past.

"Beloved, I've been waiting for you to see that you are above and not beneath. I have provided all you need for health and godliness.

"You must learn to discern my voice from the enemy's. I do not accuse you; I paid for your sin so you don't have to stand condemned. Shake it off like changing a dirty robe. Now put on the robe of righteousness that has your name on it.

"Like Joseph's robe of many colors, I have designed something especially for you. You will reflect my glory when you wear it as others see what I have done for you. I have set you apart so that my love can be shed abroad. Let my light shine through you."

Deuteronomy 28:13-14, John 10:3-5, Matthew 5:16, Isaiah 61:10

Assignment:

What have you been taught about spiritual authority?

_____

_____

Describe a crisis of belief in your life.

_____

_____

How has God revealed truth to you through His word, dividing between your soul and spirit?

_____

_____

Final thoughts:

The physical man operates in the world where Satan is god. God is God in the spirit world, and that is where we have been delegated the authority of Jesus.

Lesson 10:
Walk in the Power of the Holy Spirit

Satan tried to tempt Jesus to doubt (Matthew 4:1-10).

Satan will try to make us doubt God, so it's important to know the Word. We need to know when Satan is distorting truth by misapplying the scriptures. Jesus always used scripture against him, but in order for us to defend and protect ourselves in a like manner, we must know what the Word says.

The sword belongs to the Spirit, but we do the wielding against the enemy. The Holy Spirit will be the power behind it causing it to penetrate the target. Scripture may seem to be just words on a page until the Holy Spirit brings it to life. He will make it alive in our hearts *and* when it comes out of our mouths. If we ask, He will give us wisdom in how to use it.

Jesus is the Word; it is because of His power that we are empowered to overcome the enemy. Offensive strategy is pulling down strongholds. We do that with scripture because the Word is the sword of the Spirit. Faith comes from the spoken word (Romans 10:17; Hebrews 4:2).

Prayer: I thank you Lord that the weapons of my warfare are not carnal but mighty in you for pulling down strongholds. I cast down arguments and every high thing that exalts itself against the knowledge of God. I bring every thought captive to the obedience of Christ (2 Corinthians 10:4-5).

Looking at the elements involved in the whole armor of God discussed in the last lesson (Ephesians 10-18), our back is the only area of our body unprotected. So we shouldn't turn our backs on Satan. That is where we need each other, particularly when we are battling the enemy. (Hence the expression: "I've got your back.") In the book of Nehemiah we see some of the people building while others were battling thereby protecting those who were building.

The first time the word church is used in the New Testament is Matthew 16:18 when Jesus says, "On this rock I will build my church and the gates of Hades will not overpower it." Gates of Hades is the unseen invisible world of Satan, which will not be too strong for the church to overcome.

> *While visiting Israel we went to the region known in the Old Testament as Bashan,*(Psalms 68:22) *east of the Jordan River, now called Caesarea Philippi. At one time it was named Paneas. There is a particular cave in the area that had an underground spring that bubbled up and was thought to be the gate or portal to Hades/the Underworld. It was a cult center devoted to the god Pan. He was worshiped in natural settings such as caves.*
>
> *On each side of the cave are carved niches for the statues of deities. Beginning in the 3rd century worshipers cast sacrifices into the cave as offerings to Pan. This is the very place where Jesus told Peter that the gates of hell would not prevail against His church; they were literally standing in that place* (Matthew 16:18). *Jesus had gone miles out of His way to make that statement to the spirit world. He was saying that He would conquer the forces of darkness, and that the Church would overcome them too* (Colossians 2:15; Psalms68:18).

Jesus sees His church as building and battling, being offensive and victorious. In the Bible, gates represented ruling counsel and administrative authority. (Proverbs 31:2).

Isaiah 28:6 says gates are the place to attack because they are weaker than the walls of a city. As Christians we need to change our mindset from a defensive posture to an offensive one, and in doing so, take special care to also guard the gates to our minds.

Satan has been disarmed.

In Colossians 2:15 Jesus disarmed the spiritual forces. We see in Ephesians 6:12 *that our battle is in the heavenly realm.* God, through the cross, disarmed Satan's kingdom. As a result he has no armor left (Matthew 28:18-19). Jesus has given us His authority, which includes spiritual weapons (2 Corinthians 10:4).

Jesus said in Matthew 11:12 that the kingdom of heaven is taken by force. The Kingdom of heaven is a powerful movement where mankind is intended to reign. It will suffer violence because the enemy will try to stop it from spreading over the earth. We as Christians need to be strong and committed to take it by force We advance by taking authority over the enemy's schemes using the sword of the Spirit — the Word of God. We do this through praying with the authority Christ has delegated to us while expecting God to miraculously do what we cannot. We also need to ask to be effective in spreading the gospel message.

More weapons against the enemy:

- **Fasting** - Fasting while praying is a weapon because when we deny our flesh our spiritual ears become much sharper, and our obedience often brings breakthroughs. See examples in 1 Samuel 7:1-6; Nehemiah 1:1-6; 1 Kings 21:20-29; Acts 13:2; Isaiah 58:6-9.

- **Prayer** - We are to pray without ceasing (1 Thessalonians 5:17). There is a good reason why. When we pray, warring angels are released to fight on our behalf. Daniel and Peter's stories are examples. Read about their experiences in Daniel 9:20-23 and Acts 12:6-19. Angels are activated on our behalf just like they were for Peter and Daniel. Prayer breaks through Satan's kingdom and releases divine angelic intervention. We see in these passages of scripture why praying scripture is very powerful, and it is just as powerful today.

- **Praise** - Praise gives us strength in the battle. See Psalms149:6-9, and 2 Chronicles 20:22. The tribe of Judah, whose name means praise, always led in battle. God calls His people to "warfare worship." It's believed that Lucifer was the Archangel over worship before he fell, so it stands to reason that he would try to prevent us from worshiping because he knows it will bring victory. It restores us to the presence of God.

- **Peace** - In spiritual battles your peace is actually a weapon. It shows your confidence, and that you are not falling for the lies of the devil. The first step toward having spiritual authority over the adversary is to have peace in spite of your circumstances. When Jesus confronted the devil, He did not confront him with emotions or in fear. Knowing that the devil was a liar, He simply refused to be influenced by any voice other than God's.

  Jesus' peace overwhelmed Satan; His authority then shattered the lie, which sent demons fleeing.
  — Frances Frangipane, *The Three Battlefields*

- **Preaching and Testimony** - In the early days of the Church, believers who were dabbling in the occult were convicted when they had to burn and get rid of anything pertaining to the work of the devil. It's a problem that still exists today, and the solution is the same. If you have any occult material, get rid of it. Some people in the church today are confused about the spiritual realm, but there can be no compromise **(2 Timothy 4:1-4; Hebrews 4:12-13; Acts 19:17-19).**

- **Testimony/Witnessing** - the Holy Spirit gives supernatural power to be a witness. The act of communion is testifying about the blood of Jesus to save and heal. The blood justifies us, canceling sin's legal right to us **(Romans 5:9).** We are sanctified, redeemed, forgiven, and cleansed by the blood.

When we worship God, Satan is defeated.

Adam and Eve walked and talked with God every day, and worshiping their creator was natural for them. For us it has to be supernatural to put our entire focus on the Creator and truly worship Him. It can only come through the power of the Holy Spirit. Satan will do all he can to keep us from being free to worship God because he knows the power we have in the earthly realm as a result. What comes out of our mouths is key **(Revelation 16:13-14).** Satanic spirits operate through the mouth too. This is why we need to guard our tongues **(James 3:5-16).**

Satan was not originally created as a fallen being **(Isaiah 14:12-14).**

Before he was cast down to earth he was called Lucifer, son of the morning. He was described as perfect in wisdom and beautiful. His clothing had jewels set in gold. He was the anointed guardian Cherub. He was also called king of Tyre in Ezekiel. But his heart became filled with pride because of his beauty. His wisdom was corrupted because of his lust for power. This was before the creation of Man, so Satan was the original sinner. He was the first in creation to turn against his Creator. We know that he influenced a third of the angels to follow him in his rebellion. He wanted to supplant God's rule with his own and be worshiped like God and to be independent of God. He uses the same temptations on us: we want to be in control of our lives, independent of God. The natural man wants to be put on a pedestal and admired, seeking position and power.

God pronounced five judgments against Satan's five "I will" statements in Isaiah 14.

He said Satan would be:

1. Thrown into hell
2. Made a spectacle
3. Mocked and scorned
4. Cast out of his grave like a carcass
5. Be alone (Ezekiel 28:15-19)

Symbolism in scripture:

Some teach that these scriptures in Ezekiel 28 and Revelation 12:3-4 are talking about an earthly king, but I don't think it was only that. I think it was also referring to a supernatural being. There are principalities that rule over nations, and I believe that perhaps Satan ruled over the region of Tyre through the human king. (In Daniel the Archangel Michael talks about fighting the prince over the kingdom of Persia.) In Ezekiel 28:13 the precious stones that covered him were the same as described on the High Priest's breastplate.

He also must have had musical ability, probably for worshiping God. Verse 13 talks about the workmanship of his timbrels and pipes. It is interesting that the god Pan is depicted as being half human while having the legs and horns of a goat and is playing his panpipes. He is thought to represent Satan.

In Detroit, the Satanic Temple has a bronze statute of Satan that is half man, half goat. It shows two small children by his side, faces uplifted as if worshiping him.

Being described as the anointed cherub who covers indicates that Satan once had a high office with authority. To cover means to defend. We know there were Cherubim covering the Ark where the presence of God was seen in the Most Holy Place. Even though he had an important position, pride caused his downfall.

Through Adam's disobedience Satan became the prince of this world (John 12:31). *Because of Jesus' obedience* Satan was cast out of heaven. As a result, I don't believe he can come before God to accuse us anymore. He has no legal right to be there because Jesus has cleansed the heavens with his blood (Hebrews 9:21-24).

Revelation 12:1-13 tells us that he was cast down to earth not hell. As we discussed in lesson 8, His abode is the second heaven, which is a realm that we cannot see. The first heaven is the one we can see; the third heaven is where God's throne is, beyond the second heaven (2 Corinthians 12:2). We see a glimpse of this supernatural realm in Daniel 10:20 when the archangel describes his battle with the Prince of Persia — this is clearly not happening in the natural realm.

Satan has a chain of command and a ruling order that he governs from the second heaven (Ephesians 1:21, 6:12). Revelation 12:1-12 describes what I believe is a picture of Israel giving birth to the Messiah. I believe Satan was cast out of heaven after the resurrection in verse 10 so he can no longer come into heaven and accuse us before God. Hebrews 9:12, 21-26 says that Jesus took His blood into heaven and cleansed the heavens. Sin cannot enter heaven, therefore Satan no longer has access to the throne.

Discussion:

Revelation 12:12-13 *says the devil has come to the earth to make war. What did that look like? How did he begin to corrupt mankind?*

Satan is at war against man.

In Genesis 6 we read that *Nephilim*, which means the fallen ones or to cast down, desert or the mighty ones, came down to earth and had relations with the daughters of men. The translation of "giants" was given even though that was not correct. The Septuagint (translation of the Hebrew Bible into *Koine* Greek) says they were angels. Jude 1: 6-8 says they went after strange flesh (2 Peter 2:4-5) and did not keep their assigned boundaries. These are the angels; the ones who, after leaving their first estate went after strange flesh, and are now kept in chains.

Scripture says clearly that "spirits" are sexless, neither male nor female. In order for co-habitation to take place they had to leave their first estate or spirit existence and take a human form, i.e., *incubus* and *succubus* spirits. Genesis 19:1-3; Ezekiel 11:3; Daniel 8:15; Zechariah 2:1; Luke 1:11 and Revelation 10:1 tell us that angels can take on human form. The term used in Genesis 6:2 "sons of God," is used in Job 1:6-2:1, 38:7; Psalms 29:1 – "mighty ones", 89:6 and Daniel 3:25 to refer to "angels." Angels who were on assignment from God have special permission to take on human form, but those who are mentioned in Genesis 6:4 did it without permission.

We see in Job 1:10 and Matthew 8:29 that God had placed both boundaries and time limits on Satan. He was not allowed to go beyond those boundaries without Divine permission. If this interpretation of scripture is correct, Satan went outside the boundaries of God when he assigned fallen angels to come down and marry earthly women. However, now the boundary against him on our behalf is the blood of Jesus.

Remember that if you are a believer, he cannot cross the bloodline to harm you — unless you open the door to him. Pray for discernment to know if you have any unforgiveness or any other open door to the enemy.

As believers who are covered by the blood of Jesus we do not need to fear Satan; we are protected.

God Moment:

"My child, come away with me.

"Take a moment and come into my garden and rest. Lay your cares by the gate. I will take of them while you sit with Me. Don't be burdened with things that are temporal and seem impossible. With Me all things are possible.

"Trust Me with the things that concern you and trust Me with those whom you care about. There is nothing too hard for Me. I hear your cries and I know your heart . . . I will answer. I'm never too late.

"Take care of yourself and let me take care of those you love. Don't grow weary in well doing but come into my garden and be refreshed and renewed.

"The battle I've called you to wage is in the spirit realm, not the natural realm. The victory will come through prayer and persistence."

1 Peter 5:7; Genesis 18:14; Galatians 6:9; 2 Thessalonians 3:13

Assignment:

If you have difficulty believing you have victory over the enemy, why is that?

_____

_____

_____

What have you learned about taking authority over the enemy?

_____

_____

_____

Write out some scriptures and prayers that would be helpful for you in resisting the enemy.

_____

_____

_____

Final thought:

Because Jesus has conquered the forces of darkness the church will overcome them too.

Appendix

Useful Scriptures to Know and Pray

Openings for sickness: before the fall…after	John 8:44; Ephesians 2:1-2; 2 Corinthians 4:4; 1 John 3:10
Why do we get sick?	1 John 5:19
What do we do about that?	1 John 2:1
What about personal sin?	Psalms 32:3-4, 38:3-11; Luke 5:18-24; John 5:14; 1 Corinthians 11:29-38
Does God use sickness?	Matthew 8:17; John 11:4
What does healing look like in the Old Testament?	Exodus 15:26; Psalms 103:1-5; Proverbs 4:20-22
What about Jesus' ministry in the New Testament?	Isaiah 53:4-5; Matthew 8:16-17; Luke 7:21-22; John 5:17-21, 9:1-4
What happened to healing after Jesus died?	Matthew 10:8; John 14:12; Acts 2:43, 3:3-11, 4:29-31, 30, 5:12-16, 6:8, 8:5-8, 9:10-19
What does that look like for us today?	Mark 16:17-18; 1 Corinthians 12:28; James 5:14-16
What sicknesses can God heal?	Matthew 8:14-15, 9:2-7, 9:32-34; Luke 5:23, 8:27-35, 22:50-51; John 4:7, 5:1-11, 9:1-4; Acts 3:2, 9:32-33, 14:8

Who was healed?	Mark 5:1-20, 7:24-30; Luke 17:1, 11-19; John 4:46-54;
What must we do to receive healing? Jesus heals through natural and supernatural means. He provides the healing no matter which way it comes - dietary changes, doctors, or a touch from the Holy Spirit.	Psalms 31:10, 147:3; Matthew 9:27-31, 9:18, 15:21-28, 24:24; Mark 7:24-30, 9:1-8, 9:27-31, 10:51; John 4:46-54; 5:4-8; 1 Corinthians 11:28-30; 2 Thessalonians 2:9-10; Hebrews 3:12; James 3:16; 1 Peter 3:18
What does faith have to do with it?	Matthew 9:2,28-30; Luke 7:2-19; John 4:50; Acts 3:5-6, 28-7-9; James 5:14-16
How do we retain or walk in healing?	Exodus 15:26; Mark 2:11; Luke 7:11-17, 8:48, 8:40-56, 11:14-28,17:11-19; John 5:8; Ephesians 6:16; Hebrews 4:14

Overcoming Unbelief:

- **Hebrews 11:6** *And without faith it is impossible to please Him, for he who comes to God must believe that He is and that He is a rewarder of those who seek Him.*

- **Matthew 21:22** *And all things you ask in prayer, believing, you shall receive.*

- **2 Corinthians 5:7** *Walk by faith and not by sight.*

- **John 14: 12-14** *"Truly, truly, I say to you, he who believes in Me, the works that I do shall he do also; and greater works than these he shall do; because I go to the Father. And whatever you ask in My name, that I will do, that the Father may be glorified in the Son. If you ask Me anything in My name, I will do it."*

- **Mark 9:24** *Immediately the boy's father cried out and began saying. "I do believe; help my unbelief."*

Overcoming Pride:

- **1 Peter 5:6** *Humble yourselves, therefore, under the mighty hand of God, that He may exalt you at the proper time.*

- **Philippians 2:3-5** *Do nothing from selfishness or empty conceit, but with humility of mind let each of you regard one another as more important than himself; do not merely look out for your own personal interests, but also for the interests of others.*

- **Colossians 3:12** *And so, as those who have been chosen of God, holy and beloved, put on a heart of compassion, kindness, humility, gentleness, and patience.*

- **James 4:10** *Humble yourself in the presence of the Lord, and He will exalt you.*

Overcoming Deception:

- **Psalms 119:11** *Thy word I have treasured in my heart that I might not sin against Thee.*

- **Psalms 51:6** *Behold, Thou dost desire truth in the innermost being, and in the hidden part Thou wilt make me know wisdom.*
  John 3:20-21 *For everyone who does evil hates the light and does not come to the light, lest his deeds should be exposed. But he who practices the truth comes to the light, that his deeds may be manifested as having been wrought in God.*

- *John 14:6* Jesus said to him, "I am the way, and the truth, and the life; no one comes to the Father but through Me.

Overcoming Addiction:

- *Jeremiah 32:17* Ah Lord God! Behold, Thou hast made the heavens and the earth by Thy great power and by Thine outstretched arm! Nothing is too difficult for Thee.

- *Proverbs 28:13* He who conceals his transgressions will not prosper, but he who confesses and forsakes them will find compassion.

- *1 John 1:9* If we confess our sins, He is faithful and righteous to forgive us our sins and to cleanse us from all unrighteousness.

- *Psalm119:14* I rejoice in the way revealed by Your decrees as in all riches.

Overcoming Guilt:

- *Psalms 40: 1-3* I waited patiently for the Lord, and He turned to me and heard my cry for help. He brought me up from a desolate pit, out of the muddy clay, and set my feet on a rock, making my steps secure. He put a new song in my mouth, a hymn of praise to our God.

- *Isaiah 55:7* Let the wicked one abandon his way and the sinful one his thoughts; let him return to the Lord, so He may have compassion on him, and to our God, for He will freely forgive.

- *Romans 8:1-2* Therefore, no condemnation now exists for those in Christ Jesus because the Spirit's law of life in Christ Jesus has set you free from the law of sin and death.

- *Romans 8:38-39* For I am persuaded that not even death or life, angels or rulers, things present or things to come, hostile powers, height or depth, or any other created thing will have power to separate us from the love of God that is in Christ Jesus our Lord.

Overcoming Unforgiveness:

- *Matthew 6:14-15* For it you forgive people their wrongdoing, your heavenly Father will forgive you as well. But if you don't forgive people, your Father will not forgive your wrongdoing.

- *Mark 11:25* *And whenever you stand praying, if you have anything against anyone, forgive him, so that your Father in heaven will also forgive you your wrongdoing.*

- *Romans 14: 10,12,13* *But you, why do you criticize your brother? Or you, why do you look down on your brother? For we will all stand before the tribunal of God. Each of us will give an account of himself to God. Therefore, let us no longer criticize one another. Instead decide never to put a stumbling block or pitfall in your brother's way.*

- *James 2:13* *For judgment is without mercy to the one who hasn't shown mercy.*

- *Ephesians 4:30-32* *And don't grieve God's Holy Spirit. You were sealed by Him for the day of redemption. All bitterness, anger and wrath, shouting and slander must be removed from you, along with all malice.*

Overcoming Sexual Strongholds:

- *1 Corinthians 6:18-20* *Run from sexual immorality! "Every sin a person can commit is outside the body." On the contrary, the person who is sexually immoral sins against his own body. Don't you know that your body is a sanctuary of the Holy Spirit who is in you, whom you have from God? You are not your own, for you were bought with a price. Therefore, glorify God in your body.*

- *1 John 1:9* *If we confess our sins, He is faithful and righteous to forgive us our sins and to cleanse us from all unrighteousness.*

- *Romans 12:1* *Therefore, brothers, by the mercies of God, I urge you to present your bodies as a living sacrifice, holy and pleasing to God; this is your spiritual worship.*

- *Psalms119:9-11* *How can a young man keep his way pure? By keeping Your word. I have sought You with all my heart; don't let me wander from your commands. I have treasured Your word in my heart so that I may not sin against You.*

- *Hebrews 4:14-16* *Therefore, since we have a great high priest who has passed through the heavens-Jesus the Son of God- let us hold fast to the confession. For we do not have a high priest who is unable to sympathize with our weaknesses, but One who has been tested in every way as we are, yet without sin.*

Organization of Angels

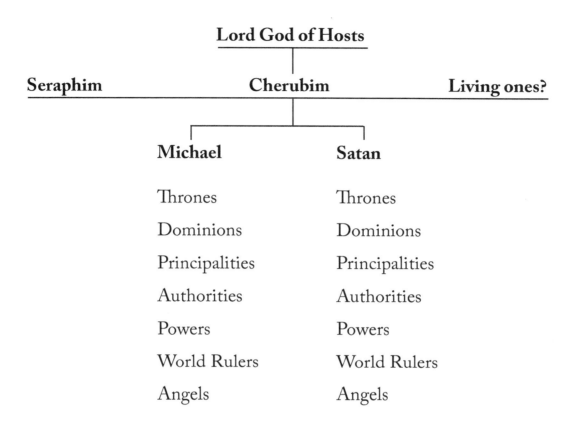

References:

Revelation, Chapters 4–5 and 12

Ezekiel, Chapter 28

Isaiah, Chapter 6

Matthew 25:41

Daniel 10:13

Romans 8:38–39

Ephesians 1:20 and 6:10

Colossians 2:15

Bibliography

Anderson, Neil. *The Bondage Breaker*: Eugene: Harvest House, 2000.

Brimm, Billye. *The Blood and the Glory*. Tulsa: Harrison House, 1998.

Frangipane, Francis. *Holiness, Truth and the Presence of God*. Cedar Rapids: Arrow Publishing, 2001.

Frangipane, Francis. *The Three Battlefields*. Cedar Rapids: Arrow Publishing, 2006.

Joyner, Rick. *There Were Two Trees in the Garden*. Wilmington: Morningstar Publications, 2006.

Leaf, Caroline, Dr. *Switch on Your Brain: The Key to Peak Happiness, Thinking, and Health*. New York: Brilliance Audio, 2014.

Lewis, C.S., *The Screwtape Letters*. New York: HarperOne, 2015.

Lord, Peter. *Hearing God*. Ada: Baker Books, 1988.

Savard, Liberty. *Shattering Your Strongholds*. Alachua: Bridge-Logos Publishing, 2001.

Whyte, H.A. *The Power of the Blood*. New Kensington: Whitaker House, 2005.

Next Steps

This is the third in a 6-part series, *Living a Supernatural Life, Naturally* by Linda Morgan. While all six parts are important, each workbook in the series can also stand alone, although they are best studied in order. The next Workbook, *Spiritual Warfare*, is especially important after the reader has been well-grounded through this Workbook on their spiritual authority in Christ.

After learning about spiritual warfare, Workbook 5, *Healing Prayer*, is a natural followup. And finally, Workbook 6, *Destiny and Inheritance*, rounds out the series of *Living a Supernatural Life, Naturally*.

CPSIA information can be obtained
at www.ICGtesting.com
Printed in the USA
LVHW052218230921
698617LV00004B/60